The Cosmopolitan

To my children
Miriam, Emily and Frederick
in this their Confirmation Year:
Luke 8.15

The Cosmopolitan World of Jesus

New Findings from Archaeology

Carsten Peter Thiede

First published in Great Britain in 2004 by
Society for Promoting Christian Knowledge
Holy Trinity Church
Marylebone Road
London NW1 4DU

British Library Cataloguing-in-Publication Data
A catalogue record for this book is available from the British Library

ISBN 0-281-05508-4

1 3 5 7 9 10 8 6 4 2

Typeset by Avocet Typeset, Chilton, Aylesbury, Bucks
Printed in Great Britain by Ashford Colour Press

It is a mistake to confound strangeness with mystery.

Sir Arthur Conan Doyle, *A Study in Scarlet*

In matters where shades of feeling are involved, it is not always easy for the historian to be as definite as he could wish.

P. G. Wodehouse, *Blandings Castle*

Contents

1 *The Desert Lives: An Introduction*

These fragments I have shored against my ruins.
T. S. Eliot, *The Waste Land*

And he withdrew himself into the wilderness.
Luke 5.16

Halfway through the Nicene Creed, we encounter a strange name: 'Crucified also for us under Pontius Pilate'. Pilate who? An obscure Roman prefect, mentioned by his Jewish contemporary Philo of Alexandria, a philosopher and diplomat, as a wicked opponent of the Jews? An evil administrator who ruthlessly killed thousands of Jews and Samaritans, as we read in the writings of the Jewish-Roman Pharisee, ex-general and historian Flavius Josephus? A high-ranking official mistakenly called 'procurator' by the Roman historian Tacitus, who holds him responsible for the crucifixion of a certain Jesus, some seventy years after the event? A man who calls himself 'praefectus', prefect, on an inscription discovered at Caesarea marking the dedication of a building to his emperor, Tiberius? Pontius Pilate would be a mere footnote to the history of the Roman Empire if he had not decisively influenced the history of mankind by ordering the execution of the Messiah Jesus and if he had not, for this reason, made it into the pages of the four most successful, most widely distributed historical writings ever published: the New Testament Gospels.

But why is he in the Nicene Creed? When its original version was conceived, in the early fourth century, Emperor Constantine was present at the Council of Nicaea, and he could easily have insisted on a more conventional solution: Jesus was born under Augustus, he was crucified under Tiberius. It would have been a straightforward imperial chronology, a framework without any deeper implications. By insisting on Pilate, the emperor and his bishops achieved a signal effect: they made sure that people understood the reality of politics and responsibilities. World history, Roman history was always also regional and local history. The representative of the emperor was in charge, and no one else. This is what the creed tells us. And thus it was another Roman

1

emperor, Constantine, who insisted on a twofold message: the Christ of Faith, the one proclaimed in the creed, must not be separated from the Jesus of History. And if you want to apportion blame for the death of Jesus the Christ, do not accuse the Jews. It is not the high priest Caiaphas or the Sanhedrin who are mentioned in the creed, but the Roman prefect Pontius Pilate.

Both messages have been widely neglected. The past one hundred years of New Testament research have been marked by the attempt to drive a wedge between the Jesus of History and the Christ of Faith. With it came the claim that the Gospel authors were not even interested in writing history, a palpable falsehood which has nonetheless acquired almost dogmatic status. And as for the emperor, he shouldered Roman responsibility in the Nicene Creed for the death of Jesus, but there has never been any genocidal anti-Italianism. Instead, ever since the mid-second century, we have had a hatred of the Jews as 'murderers of God' which has distorted and almost destroyed the truth that Christianity, if anything, is Jewish.

In this book, we will trace this real world of Jesus and his time, from Jews like the playwright Ezekiel to a Roman satirist called Petronius; from a scholarly Pharisee called Sha'ul, a.k.a. Paul, to Poppaea, the pro-Jewish wife of Emperor Nero; from fish caught in the Sea of Galilee, pickled at Magdala (Migdal) and exported to the imperial court in Rome, to the artistry of one of the greatest authors of Hellenistic literature, a certain Mark; from a young carpenter at Nazareth who helped his adoptive father rebuild Sepphoris (Zippori), the capital of Galilee, to the ascended Messiah who quoted the Greek dramatist Aeschylus somewhere on the road from Jerusalem to Damascus. It was a fascinating, multifaceted world, inhabited by people who left us real documents and artefacts, rediscovered by archaeologists, papyrologists, philologists and classical historians. Entering this world, we leave behind the bloodless creations of so much recent New Testament research, where alleged myths and pious imagination have replaced the insights of eye-witnesses and contemporaries.

A glance at the world of Jesus with the help of a present-day map shows a bewildering array of borders and frontiers – Israel, the Palestinian Territories, the areas under military administration, Egypt, Jordan, Syria, Lebanon. Even the first journey of Jesus, of the young child not yet two years old, would demand detailed planning and visa applications today. A spontaneous flight into Egypt? Not really an option in the early twenty-first century, whereas back in the late first century BC, when Jesus was born, all these countries were administrative districts, provinces, within the Roman Empire. Emperor Augustus had created the 'Pax Romana', the Roman Peace which, for the first time, made the seas safe for travellers (no pirates – Augustus himself was particularly proud of this achievement) and which improved the magnificent overland routes. Building projects, often sponsored by wealthy citizens, landed gentry and vassal rulers, produced further roads and new harbours. Trade with regions which did not belong to the empire, such as Ethiopia/Nubia, Persia and India, facilitated the spreading of religious 'merchandise'. Foreign religions like Zoroastrianism or the Mithras cult reached Rome, and less than half a century later, the Christian faith was brought to every province along the same roads and via the same harbours. There is no prima facie reason, for example, to rule out the historicity of the second-/third-century stories about the Apostle Thomas and his successful missionary journey to India. Even Britain may have been reached by Christian merchants soon after the conquest under Emperor Claudius in AD 43 – although there is no solid evidence to substantiate the legend of Joseph of Arimathea at Glastonbury. In general terms, it can be said that Christianity spread early and fast within the Roman Empire and wherever the Romans had established trade links.

And as far as Egypt was concerned, those trade links had prospered long before Roman times. In fact, just south of Bethlehem, there was an inn for travellers between Egypt and Judaea mentioned in the Old Testament (Jeremiah 41.17). Theologians may regard Jesus' first journey merely as a story meant to symbolize a kind of repeated salvific history – 'We are the Holy Family, and thus we have to go to Egypt, where Joseph did, and, again symbolically, where Jesus will return like a second Moses' – but to the historian, it all is much more down to earth. Threatened by Herod – and let it be said in passing that there is not a single solid scholarly reason to doubt the infanticide at Bethlehem – and warned just in time, Joseph, Mary and Jesus leave Bethlehem along a caravan route which would get them out of Herod's territory almost immediately, south-west towards Egypt, via Beersheba, the ancient city of Abraham. Here, in Beersheba, people knew where to find thriving Jewish communities in Egypt. It was a journey through the Negev and Zin deserts, following the meandering wadis, from oasis to

3

oasis, until they reached a region of the Roman Empire with more than one million Jewish inhabitants. At Alexandria, Egypt boasted the largest Jewish community anywhere outside Palestine. Philo, the greatest Jewish philosopher of the time, lived here; and two hundred years earlier, Alexandrian Jews had helped to produce the first complete translation of the Hebrew Bible into the Greek, the so-called Septuagint. Another city with a sizeable Jewish community, not far from the River Nile, was Hermopolis Magna. Later Christian tradition has it that it was here where the family settled. And here, in the arid, desert-like region of Hermopolis Magna, rubbish heaps were discovered last century with numerous hoards of ancient manuscripts, among them one of the oldest New Testament fragments ever found: a rare parchment manuscript, with fragments from Matthew's and Luke's Gospels, dated to *c.* AD 275.[1]

Today, it is no longer hidden in the desert, but among the lists of New Testament manuscripts. One of many strange decisions of the editors of the standard edition of the Greek New Testament, the 'Nestle–Aland', was the preference given to texts on papyrus, irrespective of their age or quality.[2] There are now 116 such papyri, identified by the letter P and a number. Anything written on papyrus is assumed to be of special value, deserving a special category. But the New Testament lists mislead their users by implying that a papyrus is more valuable than a parchment script. It is not. The material does not tell us anything about the age or quality of the text written on it. In fact, one of the oldest, if not the oldest surviving manuscript of the book of Acts is a parchment, from *c.* AD 180.[3] Hidden in the vast morass of listed uncial manuscripts, with the number 0189, it is one of four existing parchments which were written before the watershed period when Constantine the Great Christianized the empire and organized the systematic editing process of the whole Greek Bible in the decades after AD 313. Parchment 0189, like the other three, was relegated to the immense group of so-called 'uncials' or 'majuscules'. It is a useless and misleading differentiation. All the New Testament papyri are 'uncials', too: in other words, they were all written in capital, upright letters. There is a later group of manuscripts, in small letters and cursive writing, the so-called 'minuscules', but they do not surface until the Middle Ages. Our learning curve begins at Hermopolis Magna, where the fragmentary parchment 0171 with Matthew and Luke was discovered, and where Jesus may have stayed with Mary and Joseph. There is more to the world of Jesus than we imagine, and parchment fragments from the sands of Egypt, leather scrolls from the caves near the Dead Sea and papyri from Herculaneum all belong to this multifaceted world which we are only just beginning to understand. When trying to learn about the customs, the traditions and the conditions of the period in which the historical Jesus and his first followers lived and worked, we have to leave fixed categories and methodologies behind. By the same token, we will take every discovery seriously in its own right. Thus, we will eventually be able to understand events and developments in a broader context. And sometimes, later documents do shed light on earlier events.

Somewhere in the Egyptian desert, not far from the Dishna Plain, a Bedouin called Hasan from Abu Mana Bahari discovered a stack of ancient manuscripts. It was in July 1952, only five years after the discovery of the first Qumran Cave near the Dead Sea. He gave some of them away, used others to light his water-pipe or simply to enjoy the aromatic fragrance of burning papyrus, and was surprised when staff from the Coptic Museum of Cairo, who had heard rumours about his discovery, arrived at his tent and wanted to confiscate his find. By then, the manuscripts had reached the house of a Coptic priest. The officials respected the sanctity of the priest's house, and thus he was free to look for potential buyers on the world market. Some of the papyri were eventually acquired by the Chester Beatty Collection in Dublin; others found their way to the private library of the Swiss collector Martin Bodmer at Cologny near Geneva. After Bodmer's death, his vast collection of ancient manuscripts, incunabula and first editions became a public foundation. They include such famous New Testament codices as P66, an almost complete copy of John's Gospel dated to *c.* AD 150, and the equally famous and only slightly younger P75 with Luke and John, as well as a copy of Martin Luther's Ninety-Five Theses and a Gutenberg Bible. Researchers from all over the world have been working with this treasure trove. One day, it was noticed that one tiny papyrus fragment from the sands of Egypt had remained unedited. I was asked to publish it and went to Cologny.

At first sight, it was just a job to be done, preparing for publication what was supposed to be, at the time, the only unedited New Testament papyrus. Another scholar, Rodolphe Kasser of Geneva University, had found the scrap among the leaves of Bodmer Codex XVII, a fragmentary seventh-century manuscript with parts of Acts, James, 1 and 2 Peter, 1, 2 and 3 John and Jude. It is a very interesting codex in its own right, having as it does the first history of the Church, Luke's book of Acts, followed by all of the letters with the exception of Paul's letters and the anonymous letter to the Hebrews. In New Testament manuscript lists, it has the papyrus number P74.[4] Kasser had suggested that the tiny scrap, measuring 3.7 by 2.1 centimetres, with four letters on the recto, the front, and five on the verso, the back, and minute remnants of some further letters, may belong to Matthew's Gospel. It was a suggestion which persuaded the compilers of Greek New Testament papyrus lists to call it P73, even though it remained unpublished and inaccessible to potential readers. Finally, when I started to work on it, the board of the Fondation Martin Bodmer named it 'Bodmer L' ('L' = Latin for 50).[5] It soon turned out that three of the four letters on the recto were the Greek word *ouk*, which means 'not', and that the five letters on the verso read *staur*. Assuming a New Testament context, the two sides could be identified as Matthew 25.43 and 26.2–3. The *staur* on the back was the first syllable of *staurōthēnai* in Matthew 26.2, 'to be crucified'. And this is what both passages say, if completed:

> I was a stranger and you did not invite me in, I needed clothes and you did not clothe me, I was sick and in prison and you did not look after me. (Matthew 25.43, NIV)

> 'As you know, the Passover is two days away – and the Son of man will be handed over to be crucified.' Then the chief priests and the elders of the people assembled in the palace of the High Priest, whose name was Caiaphas . . . (Matthew 26.2–3, NIV)

What then is so interesting about this papyrus fragment? After all, it is very late – the end of the sixth century AD (the date given for P73 and P74 in New Testament lists, the seventh century, is wrong) – it is very small and it is very insignificant as far as its textual nature is concerned: no variants anywhere, everything is exactly as we know it from many other manuscripts of Matthew's Gospel. But it was possible to establish that the scribe who wrote this P73 of Matthew was the same man who had written the much bigger codex P74. And there, a sufficient number of characteristic traces remain to identify the scribe as a Copt, an Egyptian Christian, writing not in one of the Coptic dialects, but in

Greek. At this juncture, the matter suddenly becomes interesting again. This tiny fragment preserves words from the famous speech of Jesus on the Mount of Olives, about the signs of the end of the age, and our surviving passage on the recto comes from the very end of this apocalyptic address. Days before his crucifixion, the text takes us back to the desert experience of the young child Jesus, turning the scribe from a nondescript copyist into a real-life Copt with a history. According to one of their ancient traditions, the Copts are heirs to the people who received Jesus, Mary and Joseph after they had escaped from Herod's tentacles. They see themselves as the first Christians outside Jewish territories, as the first who gave refuge to the Messiah. And thus our Coptic scribe reached the final passage of Jesus' speech on the Mount of Olives with confidence and pride. The Lord predicts that he will return as judge, and he will divide the peoples into two groups. Speaking of himself in the third person, as 'the King', he praises those on his right:

Come, you who are blessed by my Father; take your inheritance, the kingdom prepared for you since the creation of the world. For I was hungry, and you gave me something to eat; I was thirsty and you gave me something to drink, I was a stranger and you invited me in. I needed clothes and you clothed me, I was sick and you looked after me, I was in prison and you came to visit me. Then the righteous will answer him, 'Lord, when did we see you hungry and feed you, or thirsty and give you something to drink? When did we see you a stranger and invite you in, or needing clothes and clothe you? When did we see you sick or in prison and go to visit you?' The King will reply, 'I tell you the truth, whatever you did for the least of these brothers of mine, you did for me.'

Let us assume that the Coptic scribe will have been pleased and grateful when he reached this passage. After all, his ancestors had been among these righteous people, and they had even sheltered, fed and clothed Jesus himself. There was no reason to assume that they had not shown the same hospitality to other visitors and neighbours in need. But the parable continues, presenting the opposite case:

Then will he say to those on his left, 'Depart from me, you who are cursed, into the eternal fire prepared for the devil and his angels. For I was hungry and you gave me nothing to eat, I was thirsty and you gave me nothing to drink . . .'

7

And then, immediately afterwards, there is the passage preserved on our papyrus:

> I was a stranger and you did not invite me in, I needed clothes and you did not clothe me, I was sick and in prison and you did not look after me.

The Coptic scribe of P73, more than any other reader of these lines, may still have felt at ease. As he had gathered from the first half of the parable, he and his people were safe. And yet, once more the parable continues:

> They also will answer, 'Lord, when did we see you hungry or thirsty or a stranger or needing clothes or sick or in prison, and did not help you?' He will reply, 'I tell you the truth, whatever you did not do for one of the least of these, you did not do for me.' Then they will go away to eternal punishment, but the righteous to eternal life.

It does not sound quite like politically correct theology. Eternal punishment is not a message in tune with modern expectations of a comfortable religion, but this and the call to repent – the very first message in the earliest Gospel (Mark 1.4) – are inalienable parts of the gospel message, and they have always been understood in this light. The one word on the recto of P73, the Greek *ouk*, the final 'not' of Matthew 25.43, is written in clear, carefully drawn letters. At this stage, the scribe may have thought that he and the Coptic Christians of Egypt were not affected by Jesus' judgement. And then the fragment breaks off, only to continue on the back with a later passage from chapter 26. If we fill the gap by looking at the edited text of the Greek New Testament, we know what follows. And what about the Coptic scribe? Like attentive readers today, he should have grasped the punchline. There is a recipe, a safe way, and it is the way of Christ: doing to others, to everyone without differentiation, what we would be prepared to do for Jesus himself. This is the Coptic lesson, as it were, embodied in the few words in papyrus P73: the past merits of one's ancestors do not count. The history of early Christianity, the roots of a heritage which has survived in documents, archaeological discoveries, and broken pieces of manuscripts, potsherds and inscriptions, becomes alive for us if we see the people behind the artefacts and the challenge of a message which is as topical today as it was two thousand years ago in the Holy Land or fourteen hundred years ago in the Egyptian desert. Papyrus Bodmer L, P73, is one of the tiniest New Testament fragments ever found, and yet, because of what it still says to us, it remains a direct link to the Egyptian desert years of Jesus and to his message on the Mount of Olives.

Sometimes, the broader context which we encounter in the historical traces may open up unexpected vistas. There is, for example, one large part of the ancient world where the Romans never settled and never traded, and where the Christian message never got a footing until the Middle Ages: central and eastern Europe north of the River Main and east of the Rhine. This was because of a single disastrous defeat suffered by the Romans 21 years before the death and resurrection of Jesus, at a site called Kalkriese not far from the German city of Osnabrueck, in AD 9, when Augustus was emperor. Modern research has confirmed that Jesus was born under Emperor Augustus (cf. Luke 2.1), while Herod was still alive (Matthew 2.1), i.e. before 4 BC, and that the date was the winter of 7 BC rather than the year 0, which does not exist anyway – a miscalculation made in the early Middle Ages.[6] By the year of Jesus' birth, Augustus had acquired a new title: on his orders, the Roman Senate had made his murdered adoptive father Julius Caesar a *Divus*, a divine or deified being. At a stroke, Augustus became a *Filius Divi*, a 'Son of the Divine One'. In Greek, even more explicitly, he was a *Huios Theou* – a 'Son of God', which is precisely how in Luke's Gospel, only a few verses before Augustus is mentioned, the angel Gabriel speaks to Mary of the unborn Jesus (Luke 1.35). Thus, the decisive battle at Kalkriese is very much situated in New Testament times, and indeed some of the Roman coins found at the battle site show a portrait of Augustus with the text 'FDIVIPATERPATRIAE': 'Filius Divi, Pater Patriae', Son of the Divine One, Father of the Fatherland.

And even more biblical history is involved. The Roman general who lost the battle, three of his legions, all the auxiliary troops, and his own life (he committed suicide when everything was lost), was a certain Publius Quinctilius Varus. Years before Augustus became proconsul in 'Germania', he had made Varus legate of Syria. And in this capacity, he brutally suppressed the Jewish revolt in Galilee and Judaea after the death of Herod the Great in AD 4. Flavius Josephus tells the story in his *Jewish War* (2.39–84), and he mentions that Varus crucified some two thousand of the revolutionaries. His troops occupied and burnt down

9

the city of Sepphoris and sold all its inhabitants into slavery. At that time, Mary, Joseph and the three-year-old Jesus were living a mere four miles from Sepphoris, at Nazareth. And when, several years later, Sepphoris was rebuilt by Herod Antipas with imperial permission, more beautiful than ever and elevated to the rank of capital city of Galilee, Joseph and the young Jesus, God's own 'Son of God', as it were, commuted from Nazareth to help rebuild the city. As builders and craftsmen, this one and only major building site in the vicinity kept them in employment for many years. This, at any rate, is what scholars have suggested, and they have added the assumption that Jesus learned about city life, about the life of the poor and the wealthy, the pious and the hypocrites, the landowners and the bankers, in those years as a builder (which is what the Greek word for 'carpenter' in the Gospels really means) at Sepphoris.

Thus, both Augustus and Varus link the history of Galilee and Judaea at the time of the birth and formative years of Jesus with that incident in AD 9 which was to determine the landscape of Christian Europe for almost eight centuries. In AD 7, Augustus appointed his successful and trusted relative Varus (who was married to his grand-niece Claudia Pulchra) legate of the Rhine Army. It was an appointment of the highest strategic importance. To begin with, Germanic tribes repeatedly invaded the Gallic provinces of the Roman Empire west of the Rhine, which was irritating enough; but the Romans also wanted new territories in the east, towards the River Elbe and beyond. The tribes over there were of no particular interest to them, but the area was famous for its arable soil (as it still is today). Grain was what the empire needed, and here it could be found. The first forays had been successful. One man in particular had led the Roman legions successfully into the East: a certain Tiberius, who was to become emperor and 'Son of God' after the death of Augustus in AD 14, and whose prefect Pontius Pilate crucified Jesus in AD 30. But the Germanic tribes did not give in. The Cherusci had a war-chief called Arminius, trained in Rome, and reliable enough to be granted Roman citizenship and equestrian rank. From a Roman perspective, he was a knight and citizen turned traitor, but from a Germanic perspective, he became a liberator when he organized an alliance of several tribes and lured Varus with his Roman legions into a well-prepared ambush in a forest between a hillside and a moor. Recent excavations, based on the discovery of coins and lead slingshots by an officer stationed with British Forces in Germany, Major Tony Clunn, have yielded amazing evidence – weaponry, artillery equipment, the silver mask of an officer's face helmet, and, in particular, the barricades constructed by Arminius and his men which demonstrate the strategic skill of the attackers.

Since Arminius had been trained by the Romans, his victory is certainly one example of a pupil surpassing his master. More than 20,000 Romans, half of the Rhine Army, died in that battle. Augustus was in the depths of despair, and we are told by Roman historians that he grew a beard and banged his head on the walls of his palace for weeks on end. The remaining five years of his reign were overshadowed by this catastrophic defeat which ended his hopes of conquering all of central Europe. His cry 'Quinctili Vare, legiones redde!', 'Quinctilius Varus, give me back my legions!', became proverbial.[7] Later, under Emperor Tiberius, new attempts were made to conquer these regions. His adoptive son Germanicus reached the battle site in AD 15 and buried what was left of the fallen soldiers. But even Germanicus failed to subdue the Germanic tribes. He lost skirmish after skirmish, and in one battle, he nearly met the same fate as Varus, at the hands of Arminius. The Romans realized that they had met their master in their disciple. In AD 17, nine years before Pontius Pilate became prefect of Judaea, Emperor Tiberius finally gave up. The eastern border of the empire was fortified by a so-called 'Limes' – the continental equivalent to Hadrian's Wall a century later.

If anything, such perspectives help us to understand that the world of Jesus was not confined to a forgotten corner of the Roman Empire. The people we encounter there were actors on the stage of the imperial world. And so were their languages, their cultural backgrounds and their political aspirations. Surprisingly perhaps, such insights are not entirely new. Oscar Wilde, a writer not to be found among the usual suspects in matters theological and biblical, had this to say in 1897, in his *De Profundis*:

> When one returns to the Greek, it is like going into a garden of lilies out of some narrow and dark house. And to me the pleasure is doubled by the reflection that it is extremely probable that we have the actual terms, the *ipsissima verba*, used by Christ. It was always supposed that Christ talked in Aramaic. Even Renan thought so. But now we know that the Galilean peasants, like the Irish peasants of our own day, were bilingual, and that Greek

was the ordinary language of intercourse all over Palestine, as indeed all over the Eastern world. I never liked the idea that we only knew of Christ's own words through a translation of a translation. It is a delight to me to think that as far as his conversation was concerned, Charmides might have listened to him, and Socrates reasoned with him, and Plato understood him.[8]

More than one hundred years later, modern research has confirmed Wilde's portrait of a multilingual, multifaceted world with documents which give us the real Jesus. These are the writings of authors who were at home in Hebrew, Aramaic and Greek. Passages where Jesus spoke Greek – such as in his dialogue with the Syro-Phoenician woman which is introduced explicitly as Greek-speaking (Mark 7.26; unfortunately, most translations miss the point) and passages where his Aramaic words were translated into Greek (such as in the Sermon on the Mount) can be regarded as trustworthy not least because the authors were at home in all these idioms and did not have to translate an Aramaic saying with a dictionary on their desk. And yet, we have to admit that our knowledge is fragmentary. We know less than the contemporaries of Jesus knew. Some scholars assume that only 6 per cent of all biblical sites have been excavated, and only up to 10 per cent of all manuscripts have survived. We are piecing together a mosaic. And the test for any reconstruction of events and lives from antiquity can be seen in the ability of the scholar to use all the available evidence in an attempt to rebuild the structure. One should be wary of theories which omit known elements of circumstantial evidence that do not fit a preconceived hypothesis. 'These fragments I have shored against my ruins', wrote T. S. Eliot in *The Waste Land*. The ruins of that culture are not beyond reconstruction. Returning to the world of Jesus, to the culture and to the knowledge of his time, crossing borders with him, we may find the inspiration to persevere in our own quest for a Christian culture which is built on the solid groundwork of the sources.

2 An Evening at the Theatre:
At Home with Jesus

As a general rule, the interpretation that solves the most problems
or accounts for the greatest percentage of the evidence is probably
the correct one.

Jodi Magness, *The Archaeology of Qumran and
the Dead Sea Scrolls* (Grand Rapids: 2002), p. 14

I saw a light from heaven, brighter than the sun, blazing around me
and my companions. We all fell to the ground, and I heard a voice
saying to me in Aramaic: 'Saul, Saul, why do you persecute me? It
is hard for you to kick against the goads.'

Acts 26.13–14

A holy and wealthy background

Recent excavations at Nazareth have produced some surprising results.
Elias Shama, a businessman and owner of Cactus, a coffee and gift shop
in Nazareth, had begun to dig a cellar underneath his shop, and stumbled
upon the remnants of a Roman bath, with floor tiles, hypocaust and water
channels. It is located next to 'Mary's Well', a structure with first-century
origins which Orthodox Christians regard as their traditional site of the
Annunciation, preferring it to the Byzantine and Crusader tradition at
today's Church of the Annunciation. Had Mary bathed here, and if so,
why not Jesus himself? Revolutionary questions – after all, it is common
knowledge that Jesus was brought up in a poor carpenter's family, in a
tiny village in the middle of nowhere. Archaeologists and historians were
invited to check the evidence, and they came to conflicting conclusions.

Tzi Shacham, an archaeologist at the Museum of Antiquities in Tel
Aviv, could only identify Crusader traces, dating the bath to the twelfth
century. The problem with this assessment is obvious: as Crusader
experts know, the medieval knights did not copy Roman architecture
when they built baths. They may have reused earlier Roman buildings,
and made them their own, adding Crusader elements, but if and where

they did so, the basic groundwork remained Roman. Stephen Pfann, president of the University of the Holy Land in Jerusalem, declared that the 'Roman'-period portion of Nazareth only covered a small area around the modern Basilica of the Annunciation and did not extend to the site of Elias Shama's souvenir shop.[1] But the so-called Mary's Well, which defines the area of the newly discovered baths, was part of Nazareth at the time of Jesus, and the well may even have been the town's main water source. Pfann's argument is circular, anyway: if a new discovery can be dated beyond dispute to the early first century, then the old theory must give way. It is always bad scholarship to declare an older hypothesis superior to fresh evidence.

The Israel Antiquities Authority's investigators began by assuming the structure was an Ottoman building, dated to the mid nineteenth century. Then they checked the channels, the hypocaust system and the 'cold room' (the 'frigidarium'), established their Roman origins and declared that a further bath found underneath was not just Roman, but early Roman – first century BC. Dror Bashad, head of the Authority's northern department, describes it as a bath-house of 'at least the Roman period'. Finally – so far – the archaeologist Richard Freund, Professor at the Maurice Greenberg Center for Judaic Studies at Hartford University, Connecticut, pointed out that a medieval Jewish pilgrim, Rabbi Moshe Bassola, visited Nazareth and wrote: 'We came from Kfar Kana, arriving the next day in Nazareth, where the Jesus of the Christians lived. The citizens told me that there existed a hot bathhouse where the mother of Jesus immersed herself.' In other words, they were not talking about a 'mikveh', a purifying bath (which was never hot), but probably about a structure like the one now excavated. Roman baths included a 'caldarium', the hot bath. And this rabbi was educated enough to appreciate the difference. Known as Moses ben Mordecai Bassola, he lived from 1480 to 1560 in the Italian city of Ancona and was one of the most influential Jewish scholars of his time.

A persistent local tradition, and the first archaeological traces: it all suggests a fascinating addition to our picture of Nazareth at the time of Jesus. Obviously, it is too early to publish final results – this may take another year or two – but it is an opportune moment to ask ourselves what we could have and should have known about Nazareth, anyway. For admittedly, some of the surprise, and some of the first rejections of the find, were based on the widespread assumption that Jesus' Nazareth was an impoverished settlement of perhaps 150 to 200 people, where farmers and carpenters scraped a living. Archaeological evidence from previous excavations had suggested that there were extensive olive groves and vineyards, well-built, lived-in caves, and simple but solidly built stone houses. The Via Maris, in those days the most important trade route linking Syria with Egypt, passed nearby, and thus the people from Nazareth were in frequent contact with international merchants, both selling and buying goods. Joseph was a *tektōn*, the Greek word for a builder which we still recognize in the English word 'architect', the 'arch-builder'. Wood was scarce in those parts of Galilee, and so our traditional translation 'carpenter' is misleading. He would have built houses – or indeed caves – rather than furniture. Was there enough to do in Nazareth for people like him and his adopted son Jesus (himself called a *tektōn* in Mark 6.3), once the baths had been built? A number of scholars have suggested a striking answer: Joseph and Jesus probably worked at the magnificent building site of Sepphoris, earning a sizeable income.[2] The new capital of Galilee, Sepphoris (Zippori), rebuilt after its destruction in 4 BC, was only four miles away. The city had been destroyed by the Romans, when a regional uprising after the death of Herod the Great was brutally suppressed. With imperial permission, Herod Agrippa began to rebuild it, as a model city of Graeco-Roman culture, where observant Jews and wealthy Romans were supposed to live peacefully together. Greek was their common language – in fact, Galilee had long been bilingual.

Such a magnificent building project for a growing population attracted (and demanded) experienced craftsmen. Thus, it appears to be the natural conclusion that Joseph and Jesus commuted from Nazareth to the building sites of Sepphoris. Admittedly, it is a conclusion derived from external data: Sepphoris is not mentioned in the New Testament. But historians have learned to avoid hasty assumptions; they know that absence of evidence must never be mistaken for evidence of absence. The careful analysis of contemporary sources, inscriptions, coins or, in other words, all the different forms of archaeological discoveries from a given period and region must be taken into account, even if the primary source – in our case the New Testament – does not provide the desired details. The Gospels do not claim to present a complete record of their hero's youth. Snippets of information have to suffice until the beginning of Jesus' public career. Similar 'omissions' are common in other ancient biographies. Unlike today, readers did not expect to be informed about the period before the beginning of a protagonist's public activity. Suetonius, the great Roman biographer, for example, who was born in AD 70, the year of the destruction of Jerusalem and the Temple, chooses his details almost at random: in his biography of Caesar, the first of his imperial 'lives', he begins with the sixteen-year-old who has just lost his father; in his biography of Augustus, on the other hand, he traces the origins of the family. In our case, thanks to archaeology, we know at least that Nazareth never was a backwater. And those who lived there were not cut off from the world – to the contrary, the political, economic and religious world of the Roman Empire was all around them, and exerted its influence on everyday life.

In any case, there are unmistakable traces of Jesus' practical experience as a *tektōn*. Read, for example, the parable of the wise and foolish builders in Matthew 7.24–29:

> Therefore everyone who hears these words of mine and puts them into practice is like a wise man who built his house on the rock. The rain came down, the streams rose, and the winds blew and beat against that house; yet it did not fall, because it had its foundation on the rock. But everyone who hears these words of mine and does not put them into practice is like a foolish man who built his house on sand. The rain came down, the streams rose, and the winds blew and beat against that house, and it fell with a great crash.[3]

Judging by the evidence, some people at Nazareth may have preferred to live in 'caves' – a few of these can still be seen behind the Church of the Annunciation – but they did not do so because they were poor. They did so because it was simply more practical. Archaeological traces show us that in these spacious, comfortable caves, the families lived in the central part and towards the back, whereas animals were kept near the entrance. Overnight, when it could get cold even in Galilee, the livestock provided a source of natural warmth. If we suppose that this was how Mary and Joseph lived, they would have felt 'at home' in the caravanserai with its 'stable', where Jesus was born in Bethlehem. But proper houses, built in stone, also existed in first-century Nazareth. A fine example is visible under the convent of the Ladies of Nazareth, in the immediate vicinity of the Church of the Annunciation. Nazareth, it seems, was a village with a mixed population, with craftsmen like Joseph, landowners and farmworkers and people who sold their produce locally, and to travelling international merchants who passed nearby, on the Via Maris. The undeniable fact that Nazareth is not mentioned in the Old Testament, nor in other contemporary sources outside the New Testament, does not contradict these conclusions: many other places which clearly existed in those days are not mentioned, either. A Roman presence in the area is safely established. In the years after 4 BC at the latest, when a Jewish revolt against the Romans after Herod's death was brutally suppressed and Sepphoris destroyed, several Roman garrisons guarded the region. To find traces of a Roman bath-house, perhaps originally built for an army detachment, on the outskirts of Nazareth cannot really come as a complete surprise. After the unsuccessful revolt against the Romans, this town, overlooking Lower Galilee, became as important for strategic reasons as nearby Japha (Yafa) – a fortified settlement two kilometres to the south-east mentioned in the writings of Josephus – had been before the uprising.[4]

If we go one step further, we may understand why Joseph and Mary had settled there in the first place. A Hebrew inscription of the late second century AD, discovered at Caesarea Maritima in 1962,[5] lists a number of priestly families, among them a family from Nazareth. The name of the town is written 'Nazara', in a Hebrew spelling which alludes to 'nezer', 'shoot' in Isaiah 11.1: 'A shoot will come up from the stump of Jesse; from his roots a branch will bear fruit. The Spirit of the Lord will rest on him'. It was a Davidic prophecy, which Christians later understood as a prophecy foretelling the coming of Jesus the Messiah. Matthew sums it up in his gospel (2.23): 'And he went and lived in a town called Nazareth. So was fulfilled what was said through the prophets: "He will be called *Nazōraīos*"' (this is the literal rendering of the original Greek). For families who were of Davidic descent, as Joseph and Mary both were, a place of that name could easily have been their home town, anyway.[6] In fact, many scholars assume that Nazareth was indeed a town of Davidic families, and that this may be the reason why a whole caravan of families from Nazareth visited the Temple together, and did not notice immediately, when they returned, that one of the many children was missing (i.e. Jesus; see Luke 2.44).

'Nazara' is an alternative spelling for 'Nazareth' in the Greek New Testament (Matthew 4.13; Luke 4.16), and in most cases, Jesus is not called 'the Nazarene'/'of Nazareth' in the Greek text of the Gospels, but 'the Nazōraīos', a spelling which contains the original allusion to 'nezer', 'shoot'. Even modern Hebrew preserves this: Christians are called 'Nozrim'. The Davidic family of Jesus, his mother and his adoptive father and their relatives, must have been aware of the old biblical connotations. The name of the town and the people who settled there are closely linked, and we may accept the conclusion of some scholars that Nazareth/Nazara was in fact originally built by ancestors of Joseph and of his wife-to-be, Mary. Some one thousand years after David, these Davidic relatives had long developed multiple branches; and regardless of their professional activities and status, they formed an elite of royal, pre-messianic descent within Jewish society. It is important to keep this in mind if one wants to do justice to the status of Joseph, Mary and others in the town of the 'nezer'. We know from the New Testament that Joseph was called a 'just one' (Matthew 1.19), a *dikaios* in Greek or *zadik* in Hebrew – an honorary title bestowed on those who knew the Torah well and obeyed it piously. And we know from the Jerusalem Talmud, the Talmud Yerushalmi, that 'builders' were highly respected and that such craftsmen were regarded as learned in Holy Scripture.[7] The human Jesus had a privileged childhood in a privileged environment, with or without Roman baths.

The family was apparently quite well to do, anyway. A document from the Babata Archive found in the 'Cave of Letters' near the Dead Sea south of En-Gedi tells us that a Roman census required all landowners to be registered in person, at a records office near the property (and as we know from the archive, 'near' could still mean a journey of several days).[8] Joseph obviously had property near Bethlehem, his home town (and another Davidic city). But why did Mary go with him? She was about to give birth, and therefore should have stayed at home. One possible reason follows from Roman law: she, too, had property of her own in the vicinity of Bethlehem, and had to go and be registered herself.[9] The document from the Cave of Letters, Papyrus Yadin 16, is an attested copy of a statement of property and a tax declaration dated 2 December AD 127. The declaration was made by a Jewish lady called Bab(a)ta. Five years later, in AD 132, she joined the Bar-Kochba revolutionaries, and when the Romans finally succeeded in putting down the revolt, many of Bar-Kochba's adherents found refuge in caves near the Dead Sea, where they were finally found and killed or simply died of starvation. When she hid in the cave, Babata took her most valuable possessions with her, jewellery and legal documents. Papyrus Yadin 16 – named after the

Israeli archaeologist Yigael Yadin, who found the cave in 1961 – was written in Greek, like Luke's Gospel, and confirms the legal language used by Luke to describe the Roman census at the time of Jesus' birth. Earlier Egyptian papyri with census documents help us to understand the continuity in the Roman system of financial administration, from the period of Augustus to the reign of Hadrian and later. What makes the Babata document so important is its origin: it comes from the Roman administration of what we call the Holy Land, not from Egypt. Babata and her husband Judanes lived in Maoza, a village south-east of the Dead Sea; the property to be declared was near Rabbath, 40 kilometres away. We read about Babata's property, inherited from her father Simon. Judanes signed the census document not as her husband, but as her guardian: at least from the first century BC, Roman law did not allow women to act in legal matters without a male guardian, who could of course be her own husband. Thus, in the case of Mary and Joseph, Joseph had to go to Bethlehem not only because of his own possessions near the town, but also because he had to countersign Mary's document as her legal guardian. According to Jewish law, a woman could inherit property if the father died without male heirs (Numbers 27.8). So we learn that Mary had a wealthy father but no brothers.

It is fair to assume that Joseph and Mary let their property, and that it included arable land which was not within easy walking distance of Bethlehem. When the 'hotels' in Bethlehem turned out to be fully booked, as other owners had also arrived in the town to be registered there, they chose the next best option, warm and safe enough for a pregnant woman. In fact, both Mary and Joseph, landowners in Judaea, could have paid for the most comfortable accommodation, had it been available. Later, when Mary and Joseph sacrifice 'a pair of doves or two young pigeons', presenting Jesus at the Temple and obeying the ritual of the cleansing of the mother (Luke 2.22–24), this should not be seen as a sign of poverty: Luke himself does not interpret the passage in Leviticus 12.6–8 in this sense. He quotes it, but without its second half, which says that these birds are an alternative sacrifice for those who cannot afford a sheep. Quite the contrary: the Davidic family consciously and humbly chose the doves, with their symbolic value as signs of God's spirit of renewal. We are reminded of the dove with the freshly picked olive leaf returning to Noah's ark (Genesis 8.11).[10] At the Temple, Mary and Joseph were confirmed in their attitude only minutes

19

later, when Simeon addressed them and proclaimed the 'Nunc Dimittis' (Luke 2.25–32) and when the prophetess Anna praised God for the birth of the redeemer of Jerusalem (Luke 2.36–38).

Returning to the discovery of the Roman baths at Nazareth, we realize that such an installation, should it really turn out to be Roman and to have been available to non-Roman inhabitants like Mary, Joseph and Jesus, would merely underline what we could have gathered from the sources anyway. The only real surprise to many may be the conclusion that Nazareth was anything but a nondescript village with a handful of poor Jews.

Formative years in a Graeco-Roman environment

Those were formative years, but there was, as yet, no public ministry. The Gospel authors, and, we may assume, their target groups, were not interested in the silent years before the calling of the first disciples. The one exception is Luke's account of the twelve-year-old in the Temple courts at Passover, debating with the teachers of the Law (Luke 2.41–50). Filling this 'gap' was a task tackled by later legendary writings, such as the *Proto-Gospel of James* and the *Infancy Story of Thomas*, texts of the late second century. They are collections of legends, although scholars debate the potential historicity of individual stories in the *Proto-Gospel* which influenced early Christian piety.[11] Both were probably written by non-Jews, but they do not contain any useful first-hand information on how a pagan society might have seen Jesus, or on how non-Jewish Christians reacted to the Jesus message in the later second century. In other words, they do not add to our portrait of the international, cross-cultural world of Jesus.

Just to convey the flavour of the *Infancy Story of Thomas*, here is one of the many miracle legends it relates, the only one which is presented in a cultural context:

And when Joseph saw the understanding of the child and his age, that he was growing to maturity, he resolved again that he should not remain ignorant of letters; and he took him and handed him over to another teacher. And the teacher said to Joseph: 'First I will teach him Greek, and then Hebrew.' For the teacher knew the child's knowledge and was afraid of him. Nevertheless he wrote the alphabet and practised it with him for a long time; but he gave him no answer. And Jesus said to him: 'If you are indeed a teacher, and if you know the letters well, tell me the meaning of the Alpha, and I will tell you that of the Beta.' And the teacher was annoyed and struck him on the head. And the child was hurt and cursed him, and he immediately fainted and fell to the ground on his face. And the child returned to Joseph's house. But Joseph was grieved and commanded his mother: 'Do not let him go outside the door, for all those who provoke him die.'[12]

We learn more about the early years of Jesus when we look at Nazareth's neighbouring town again, the new capital of Galilee, Sepphoris. It remained the capital of Galilee until AD 20, when Antipas built and elevated Tiberias, but was reinstalled in its previous position by the procurator Felix in *c.* AD 52. Life in this multicultural city left its mark on the New Testament, both in the Gospels and in Acts, even if 'anonymously'. The most striking building, just completed in the early decades of the first century AD, was the theatre.[13] It had been conceived by Herod the Great, but he died in 4 BC, before he could build it. His son Antipas took over when he rebuilt the destroyed city. With a diameter of 74 metres, the theatre had 5,000 seats, and in a city of roughly 25,000 inhabitants, this suggests a rather lively interest in drama. And it presupposes fluency in Greek, since this was the language of the theatre in the east of the Roman Empire – no Aramaic or Hebrew plays were written or performed, and Latin remained the public language of the West.

In a city with a sizeable Jewish majority, it must be taken for granted that Jews, too, attended performances. No one, not even King Herod Antipas, builds a majestic theatre when he knows that most of the population will never go there. In fact, the widespread notion that Jews did not go to the theatre is wrong. The evidence to the contrary, at least in the centuries before the destruction of Jerusalem and the Temple, is overwhelming. At Miletus, a city later visited by the apostle Paul, a row was reserved for the Jews – the inscription has survived. In literature, there is the *Letter of Aristeas*. Half legend and half history, it was written to explain the origins of the Septuagint, the Greek translation of the Hebrew Bible, and it recommends the theatre as a kind of psychological therapy. Published probably in Alexandria, in the second century BC, it has a scene where King Ptolemais II invites Jewish guests to a festive dinner and asks them questions. Here is the one that concerns us most:

Then he asked someone else: 'What should one do in one's leisure time, so as to amuse oneself?' He replied: 'It is apt and even useful for one's life if one watches decent plays and scenes from life played with dignity. For this, too, is instructive in a certain way – often, one can learn something good from what is most unimportant.'[14]

What is more, there was at least one Jewish playwright, the Greek-speaking Ezekiel the Tragedian. One might argue that Jews in the Diaspora, in Alexandria, Rome, Athens or Miletus, were more willing to enjoy the cultural benefits of pagan lifestyles than Jews in the Holy Land, but Galilee had always been more cosmopolitan than Judaea and Samaria. In addition to the theatre at Sepphoris, there was a second one in the north-west, at Caesarea Maritima, the northern port of Judaea, which had been the seat of the Roman administration since 6 BC. Here, Herod Agrippa fell ill during a public address and died soon after.[15] The theatres at Caesarea and Sepphoris have been excavated; the one at Caesarea was reconstructed and has become a venue for popular performances. But it was not just the 'Galilee of the Gentiles' – as Isaiah once famously called it (8.23) – which inspired theatre builders. In New Testament times, at least two existed south of Galilee: in Jericho and in Jerusalem.[16]

What was the standard repertoire of a theatre in the Greek-speaking east, and particularly in the Holy Land? Were the works of the only Jewish playwright whose name has come down to us, Ezekiel the Tragedian, ever performed at Sepphoris, Caesarea or elsewhere? Or to put it differently, what could Jesus and Joseph, Paul and the others have seen on stage? They were five to six centuries removed from the period of the great classics of Greek tragedy, Aeschylus (525–456 BC), Sophocles (496–406 BC) and Euripides (480–406 BC), and from the most popular authors of comedies, Aristophanes (445–386 BC) and Menander (342–291 BC). Even Ezekiel the Tragedian had long been dead – although we do not have precise dates for him, he must have written in the second century BC. But the classics lived on, and at the time of Jesus, which is commonly called the Hellenistic period, they would still have been performed. We even find traces of these plays in the New Testament: Jesus' word to Paul on the road to Damascus, 'It hurts you to kick against the goads' (Acts 26.13), is taken from Aeschylus.[17] Paul's dictum 'Bad company ruins good morals' (1 Corinthians 15.33) occurs in Euripides' play *Aiolos*.[18] Jesus, Paul and Luke could have quoted, of course, from a florilegium, an anthology of popular passages from classical plays. But given the fact that there were theatres practically everywhere Paul went, and that Jews did go to the theatre in those days, it is much more probable that he, like Luke, joined their fellow Jews and attended performances of Euripides, Menander and the others.

Eventually, tragedy lost its influence, but the Greek comic dramatist Menander remained popular enough until the early third century for readers to mistake him for the author of what turned out to be a Jewish writing, 'The Wisdom of Menander'. This text was in turn quoted at length by an anonymous Christian writer, Pseudo-Justin, in his treatise *On the Unity of God*.[19] In the first century, new types of play became popular and eventually took over the stage, both in the West and the East: the 'pantomime' and the 'mime'. The pantomime, where dancers represented mythological scenes, supported by a chorus and incidental music, was a popular art-form both in the Latin west and in the Greek east, where it was called 'the Italian dance'. Tragic themes were preferred, but some actors specialized in satiric drama or scenes from comedy. The pantomime actors often appeared in up to five different roles (and masks), and the greatest among them were highly paid celebrities. One of those players was in fact a Jew: Alityrus, 'a special favourite of Nero', as Josephus called him.[20] Mimes, on the other hand, were performances with increasingly erotic, explicitly sexual and violent scenes. Audiences loved it, and the new fashion had reached Greece and Asia Minor by the time of Peter, Paul and the other early Christian missionaries. The West was worse than the East in this respect, and many of these plays contained real-life crucifixions and rape, staged with slaves or criminals condemned to death. Female actors were asked by rapturous audiences to do a striptease at the end of a play and did so more often than not; sexual acts with animals were realistically imitated – in fact, most of the more extreme absurdities of the modern stage were part and parcel of the first- and second-century repertoire in the Roman Empire.

When these popular perversions increasingly replaced the classics, Jews and Christians discouraged the faithful from going to the theatre.[21] Novatian, not the first, but the most outspoken Christian critic, condemned the contemporary stage and at the same time realized that a positive precedent for a Christian theatre had been set in the Old Testament:

> The fact that David appeared before God as choir leader does not help faithful Christians who sit in the theatre. For David did not contort his limbs in obscene movements in order to dance a play which had sprung from Greek lasciviousness. Harps, lutes, flutes, timpani and zithers were heard in praise of God, not of a godhead's graven image.[22]

At roughly the same time, around AD 250, the so-called *Teaching of the Twelve Apostles*, the *Didascalia Apostolorum*, went a step further. In this collection of rules and admonitions, which influenced Christian practice until the Middle Ages, Christians were not only told to avoid the theatre, they were admonished not even to meet people who had been corrupted by a visit to the theatre. Much earlier, educated Romans had been equally repelled by such plays. Tacitus, the historian (AD 55–116), compared the primitive Germanic tribes to decadent Romans in his *Germania* of AD 98 and praised their way of life: 'The women lived in demure chasteness [*pudicitia*] and were not depraved by the temptations of the plays or the provocations of the banquets'.[23]

One of the most successful writers of such plays was a certain Catullus. His *Laureolus*, written in the twenties of the first century AD, and a stage 'hit' for at least a hundred years, includes the crucifixion of a thief. The text is lost, but we have the comments of four authors: the poet Martial, the satirist Juvenal, the historian Suetonius, and the Jewish historian Josephus, who saw it during a visit to Rome, in the presence of Emperor Caligula.[24] For Christian readers of Josephus, the matter-of-fact reference to the thief's crucifixion in that mime performance is remarkable, only a few chapters after his account of the crucifixion of Jesus.[25] But then again, crucifixions were an everyday event in those years, in Judaea and Samaria as much as in Rome. A Jewish observer like Josephus, who worked and wrote for the imperial family of the Flavians, could not afford to get emotionally involved.

There is, however, a somewhat macabre side to it. We have every reason to assume that the *Laureolus* was also performed in the East, as a kind of light entertainment for civil servants and Latin-speaking contingents in major garrison towns. Someone like Pontius Pilate, an ardent crucifier, would have enjoyed a performance in the theatre of Caesarea Maritima, the harbour city which served as his seat of administration. In fact, there is a link between the *Laureolus* and a scene immediately before the crucifixion of Jesus. The soldiers and officers of the Roman cohort gathered in the Praetorium – probably at the Upper Herodian Palace not far from the Temple – perform a stageworthy 'mime' when they strip Jesus naked, put a scarlet robe on him, put a reed in his right hand and a crown of thorns on his head and mock him with theatrical exclamations of 'Hail, King of the Jews!', before they spit on him, take the reed and strike him on the head, mock him again, strip him of the robe and lead him away to crucify him (Matthew 27.27–31). Such cruelty could easily have been inspired by a performance of Catullus' *Laureolus* in their home garrison of Caesarea.

The contrast between such mimes and classical theatre could not be greater, even though many comedies by Menander, or Roman authors like Plautus (254–184 BC), also contained scenes of sexual ribaldry. Those authors refrained from on-stage explicitness, however. In any case, tragedies in the classic mould left the most cruel events – the maiming or death of a hero or heroine, for example – to the imagination of the spectators and readers. The Jewish playwright Ezekiel the Tragedian walked a particularly fine tightrope in this respect. He knew that the Song of Songs could be seen as a love song in the form of a lyrical drama; he also knew that the book of Job could be understood by Greek and Hellenized Jewish readers as a tragedy in the manner of Aeschylus' *Prometheus*. These biblical books were pure dramatized literature. But staging the story of God and Moses, the exodus of the Israelites from Egypt, with actors, was a different matter altogether, in view of the Second Commandment. He took the risk in his play *Exagōgē* (Exodus), a dramatization of the first fifteen chapters of the second book of the Torah. It is his only play which has survived at least in sizeable passages: 269 lines from six scenes in the classic metre of tragedies, the iambic trimeter, have come down to us in quotes by later writers.[26] Ezekiel was audacious enough to invent scenes which are not part of the biblical story – after all, he was a creative poet. So he added such things as a magnificent monologue on the beauty of the palms and the phoenix bird at the oasis of Elim, a dream of Moses and the character of Chous, a brother of Zipporah, the wife of Moses (Exodus 2.21, 4.24–6), who – according to some interpreters – gave her name to the city of Sepphoris ('Zipporah', like 'Sepphoris', is derived from the Hebrew 'zippōn', bird; the modern Hebrew name of the location is Zippori), where Ezekiel's play may have been performed in the first century AD. Since Ezekiel emphasized the importance of Passover and the seasonal rules, one may even suggest that it was a drama to be performed in the Passover season.

Nothing much is known about Ezekiel. Since Alexander Polyhistor quotes him in about 30 BC, he must have been an author of the first century BC at the latest. Did he live in Egypt, perhaps in Alexandria, the centre of Jewish culture in the diaspora of those days? Or perhaps he was a native of Roman Palestine and wrote for Herod the Great's theatre at Caesarea? We do not know. All we have are the excerpts from his play on the subject of the Exodus.[27] Here is one of the surviving scenes, from Act III, in English prose which cannot emulate the refined elegance of Ezekiel's Greek metre:

Moses: Woe! What sign is coming towards me, from the
                  burning bush,
              Incomprehensible, and incredible to men?
              Suddenly, the bush is ablaze,
              And yet, its branches remain unscathed.
              What is this? I would like to get closer and watch the
                  miracle,
              The more-than-powerful one, for men cannot believe it.

Voice of God: Stop, my dear! Don't come closer,
              Moses, until you have untied the laces of your shoes,
              For holy is the earth where you stand.
              The voice of God it is which sends its beams to
                  you from the bush.
              Take courage, my child, and listen to my words, for
              To see my face is impossible
              For a mortal, but you can listen to my words;
              I have come for their sake.
              I am the God of your fathers,
              Of Abraham and Isaac and Jacob, these three.
              In memory of those and of my earlier promises
              I am here to save my Hebrew people,
              I who see the misery and the tribulations of my
                  servants.
              But go and explain with my words,
              First to the Hebrews, to all of them,

26

> Then to the King, the message of my commands,
> So that you may lead my people out of this country.

Moses:　I am not eloquent, and my tongue
　　　　　Does not readily find the right word and easily falters,
　　　　　　　so that my words
　　　　　Will not achieve anything before the King.

Voice of God:　I will quickly send you your brother Aaron,
　　　　　So that you may tell him everything I have told you,
　　　　　And *he* shall speak before the King.
　　　　　You belong to me, but he takes from you.

It may sound rather unexciting, but the original Greek is competent and reveals the skill of an expert dramatist. In those days, there was no Jewish theatre. Audiences were mixed, and since Ezekiel's plays were performed in public, he had to cater for 'pagan' tastes as well.[28] The way he presents God on stage – heard, but not seen – was acceptable to orthodox Jews and, at the same time, pleased a Graeco-Roman audience used to the much less subtle *Deus ex machina*, literally the god from the stage machinery: the sudden appearance of a god lowered on to the stage, with the solution to all the unresolved questions. A theatrical trick, developed by Euripides into a fine art, was reduced to an invisible voice from above by the Jewish playwright Ezekiel.

This world of the stage was close enough to be part of the world of Jesus and the Gospels. Even if we hesitate to accept the thought of the adolescent Jesus as a builder, working with his adoptive father on the construction of the new theatre in Sepphoris, and sitting among other Jews and non-Jews, like the Jews in their own row at the theatre of Miletus, when Aeschylus, Sophocles, Euripides, Aristophanes or Menander was performed, we encounter scenes which resemble the stagecraft of a Euripides in the Gospels. Mark and John in particular used this technique to create an uplifting, surprising effect. It is not difficult to read, for example, a well-known passage from John's Gospel like a scene straight from Euripides or Ezekiel. Here is John 12.20–36, where Jesus foretells his death and his subsequent glorification, set as such a scene:

The Cosmopolitan World of Jesus

Passover music. Enter some Greeks, approaching Philip of Bethsaida.

The Greeks: Sir, we wish to see Jesus.

Enter the Chorus, exit Philip. Philip returns with Andrew and Jesus.

Jesus: The hour has come for the Son of Man to be glorified. Very truly, I tell you, unless a grain of wheat falls into the earth and dies, it remains just a single grain; but if it dies, it bears much fruit. Those who love their life lose it, and those who hate their life in this world will keep it for eternal life. Whoever serves me must follow me, and where I am, there will my servant be also. Whoever serves me, the Father will honour. Now my soul is troubled. And what should I say – 'Father, save me from this hour'? No, it is for this reason that I have come to this hour. Father, glorify your name.

Silence. Then suddenly drums and thunder, noises from above.

A voice from
heaven: I have glorified it, and I will glorify it again.

Chorus I: The roar of thunder! What can that mean?

Chorus II: An angel has spoken to him!

Jesus: This voice has come for your sake, not for mine. Now is the judgement of this world; now the ruler of this world will be driven out. And I, when I am lifted up from the earth, will draw all people to myself.

Chorus I: This is to indicate the kind of death he is to die!

Chorus II: We have heard from the Law that the Messiah remains for ever. How can you say that the Son of Man must be lifted up? Who is this Son of Man?

Jesus: The light is with you for a little longer. Walk while you have the light, so that the darkness may not overtake you. If you walk in the darkness, you do not know where you are going. While you have the light, believe in the light, so that you may become children of light.

Exit Jesus.

This is just one example from many which could be printed, in modern editions of the Gospels, like scenes from a play. Many will remember Alec McCowan's staging of Mark's Gospel, in the 1980s. Using the Authorized Version, he performed the Gospel, verbatim, with nothing but a desk and a chair for his props, captivating audiences all over Britain for two hours. Scenes like Mark 6.35–41, 8.14–21 and 9.14–27 were – and are – particularly effective. In John's Gospel, the extended scene 13.31—16.33 or, shorter but no less captivating, 21.15–23, obviously appealed to readers and listeners who knew and loved the theatre.[29] In fact, the renaissance of theatrical performances in Christian Europe, after the extended lull which had been caused by Tertullian's diatribe against the theatre in his *De Spectaculis*, is due to a scene from Mark's Gospel. Tertullian famously exclaimed: 'You want to see blood? You have the blood of Christ!' And he recommended patience: the day of the Last Judgement will be the most spectacular of all dramas on the greatest of all stages, the New Jerusalem.[30] But Bishop Ethelwold of Winchester, perhaps unaware of Tertullian's verdict, or consciously ignoring him, resuscitated the theatre in AD 970. In his *Regularis Concordia*, he describes the early morning service on Easter Day. Four monks, speaking Latin, in the roles of the angel and the three women mentioned in Mark 16.1–7, act out the scene at the empty tomb:

The angel: Who are you looking for, O followers of Christ [*christi-colae*]?

The women: Jesus of Nazareth, the crucified one, O celestial one [*caelicola*].

The angel: He is not here, he is risen, as it was prophesied. Go, and proclaim that he is risen from the dead!

29

The women: Hallelujah, the Lord is risen, today is risen the mighty lion, Christ, the Son of God.

The angel: Come and see the site where the Lord was placed, Hallelujah!

The women: The Lord is risen from the tomb, he who hung for us on the cross, Hallelujah!

Ethelwold gave precise stage directions for everything that was to be done between these dialogues. At the end, the priest sang a triumphal hymn, Ethelwold's version of the *Te Deum*.[31] His Easter scene became so popular that it had to be performed outside the Benedictine abbey churches for which it was written. Eventually, extended Easter plays and passion plays were written, and public performances, in church squares and market-places, initiated a new interest in the theatre. Christian teaching, which had suppressed the theatre for more than seven centuries, assisted at its rebirth.

Links between the New Testament and the world of the theatre are tangible even in the Galilean countryside. In Mark 4.1–2, Jesus 'began to teach beside the lake. Such a very large crowd gathered around him that he got into a boat on the lake and sat there, while the whole crowd was beside the lake. He began to teach them many things in parables'. This bay has been identified by archaeologists, not far from Capernaum. It resembles the semicircle of a Graeco-Roman theatre, and experiments have shown that a man sitting or standing in a boat in the middle of the bay can be heard clearly by people even on the upper slope of this natural theatre.[32] The same phenomenon occurs on the so-called 'Mount of the Beatitudes', where Jesus preached the Sermon on the Mount. 'When Jesus saw the crowds, he went up the mountain; and after he sat down, his disciples came to him. Then he began to speak, and taught them' (Matthew 5.1–2). There are still scholars who doubt that Jesus ever preached this sermon, and the top of the hillock, where a church built in 1938 attracts tourists, must indeed be ruled out. Up there, the wind tends to blow so fiercely that one can hardly understand one's own words, let alone those of an orator a short distance away.

But some two hundred metres from the church, downhill towards Tabgha, there is a natural semicircle and an even surface which still looks just like the 'orchestra' of a Graeco-Roman stage. Anyone standing in the centre of this stage can speak quietly and will still be understood. It is the famous Epidaurus effect, known to many visitors to this ancient Greek city who have whispered centre-stage, only to find that someone in the upper rows has understood every syllable. Jesus, the skilled public speaker, knew what he was doing. It is only fair to assume that he chose the bay and the natural theatre on the hill because of his experience with stage effects. And as we have seen, the opportunity for him to gain this experience had been at his doorstep, in the theatre of Sepphoris.

Another link with the theatre is Jesus' frequent use of the word 'hypocrite', for example in Matthew 6.2: 'So whenever you give alms, do not sound a trumpet before you, as the hypocrites do in the synagogues and in the streets, so that they may be praised by others. Truly I tell you, they have received their reward.' This sounds innocuous enough at first hearing, until we examine the original Greek word, *hypokritēs*. It means actor. In the Septuagint, it had already acquired its metaphorical meaning of pretender, dissembler, hypocrite (see e.g. Job 34.30; 2 Maccabees 5.25), and in this sense, it occurs seventeen times in the Gospels, exclusively when Jesus addresses an audience and describes his opponents. But even in contemporary Greek literature, it also retained its original meaning. How did people in those days, in the absence of television, magazines and newspapers recounting the latest antics of famous actors, appreciate the double meaning of the word? From what we now know about the cultural reality of first-century Galilee and Judaea, the answer should be as obvious as it is for other regions of the Roman Empire: because they had seen actors, 'hypocrites', on stage, wearing masks and generally playing a role, pretending to be someone and something different from what they actually were. The image of the trumpet in the passage from Matthew quoted above may therefore also be understood as a hint at stagecraft. Trumpets played a role in Greek plays – they were part of the incidental music in the theatre, at public ceremonies and at games. Several types are known from literary references and archaeological discoveries: the Greek *salpinx* (straight) and *keras* (curved), and the Roman *tuba* (straight), *cornu* (curved) and *lituus* (cylindrical and curved upwards).

There is also a theological aspect to theatrical terminology in the New Testament: the word we know as 'sin', or *hamartia* in Greek. Consider one example, in Sophocles' *Antigone*. King Creon enters the scene, with the body of Haemon:

> Woe –
> The sins of the senseless mind,
> Hard and death-bringing.
> Oh you, see the slayer, and,
> Of the same blood, the slain.
> Woe is me – my wretched decisions!
> Oh child, young and dead!
> Oh! Oh!
> You died, you were torn away,
> By my, not by your false counsel. (1261–9)

Aeschylus, too, used 'sin' in this sense, for example in his *Agamemnon*, when Cassandra addresses the Chorus:

> On your oath, bear witness that I truly know
> The guilt of ancient sin in this house. (1196–7)

These passages from Sophocles' *Antigone* and Aeschylus' *Agamemnon* remind us of a statement in the letter of James, 1.14–16: 'But one is tempted by one's own desire, being lured and enticed by it; then, when that desire has conceived, it gives birth to sin, and that sin, when it is fully grown, gives birth to death. Do not be deceived, my beloved.' The philosopher Aristotle, for his part, analysed the concept of 'sin' as an element of tragedy in his *Poetics*. For him, *hamartia* is a grievous fault committed by man, wrong behaviour caused in spite of an effort to do what is right, because of the imperfection of mankind (1353a10). Sin, *hamartia*, can be followed like a thread throughout the Greek Old Testament, from Genesis 15.16 onwards, and in the New Testament, where it occurs no less than 173 times. And it helps to know that educated Gentile readers were acquainted with it from the theatre, if not from Aristotle and other philosophers (see, for example, Plato's *Laws* 660c). The outstanding skills of Jesus and the Gospel authors were not confined to their unsurpassed mastery of the Old Testament in Hebrew and Greek, and of Jewish culture with its rich heritage. Those skills also comprised the all-pervasive Graeco-Roman ways of life. The world of the theatre is one example of this cultural wealth which they exploited for the benefit of their audiences.

3 Who is Who? Emperors, Miracle Workers and Sons of God

> Do you describe a forest by describing every tree within it, or by describing the appearance and ecology of the forest as a whole?
>
> Stephen M. Wylen, *The Jews at the Time of Jesus*
> (New York and Mahwah, NJ: 1996), p. 15

> So they read from the book, from the law of God, with interpretation. They gave the sense, so that the people understood the reading.
>
> Nehemiah 8.8

Temples for a son of God

Jesus was born into a multicultural world which continued to shape the early ministry of the first Christian communities. One of the most striking aspects of this world was the inescapable presence of the Roman emperors, in their decrees, their inscriptions and their temples. Sepphoris, the city with the theatre Jesus saw, had been destroyed in 4 BC by order of Emperor Augustus, when Jesus in nearby Nazareth was three years old, and permission to rebuild it had come in 3 BC from the same emperor. Caesarea by the Sea – or 'Caesarea Maritima' – traditionally called 'Strato's Tower' – had been embellished as a magnificent seaport by Herod the Great, and its new name 'Caesarea' was of course intended to honour Caesar Augustus. In north-eastern Galilee, the other Caesarea had been known as 'Paneas', after a shrine dedicated to the Greek god Pan, but Herod's son Philippus renamed it Caesarea in honour of Augustus, the Caesar. To distinguish it from the seaport, Philippus' own name was added, and so we find it as 'Caesarea Philippi' in the Gospels (Mark 8.27; Matthew 16.13) and other sources. These Herodian renamings were not the only Roman traces in the region – both Caesareas were famous for their temples dedicated to Augustus by Herod the Great. In fact, Herod was merely following a fashion. No fewer than 37 temples were built for Augustus during his lifetime, and another 19 after his death, mainly in the Greek-speaking regions of the empire. It must be emphasized that the Latin-speaking West was more reticent toward this industry: ancient Rome did not really appreciate hero worship, kings and man-like gods, and Augustus himself played down his divine status as far as he could, not least, as Philo of Alexandria tells us, because he knew 'that the Jews, whom he received in a friendly way, despised such things'.[1] But eventually, even the Latin-speaking West followed suit; and when Vespasian was on his death-bed, in AD 79, he managed to crack one of his better jokes: 'Oh, I think I will become a God.'[2]

All Jews and Gentiles in Galilee, Judaea and Samaria were familiar with the imperial cult, and Mary and Joseph were no exception. On their way from Nazareth to Bethlehem, in the winter of 7 BC, they followed the traditional road from Galilee to Jerusalem, through Samaria (Shomron), and passed a city called Sebaste. Better known as 'Samaria', like the ancient province, it had been renamed by Herod the Great, in honour of Emperor Augustus ('Sebaste' is Greek for 'Augusta', the city 'of Augustus'). Its most magnificent site was a temple built by Herod on the summit of the acropolis, above earlier structures erected under Omri and Ahab (cf. 1 Kings 22.38–9). Herod dedicated it to Augustus and the goddess of the city of Rome, the 'Dea Roma'. For Mary, the sight of this temple would have given a political and religious perspective to something she had heard only a few months before: the angel Gabriel had visited her with the message that her son, not yet born, would be called 'the Son of the Most High' and 'the Son of God' (Luke 1.32, 35). But this was precisely what the temple in Samaria/Sebaste claimed of Augustus at the time: 'Son of God', in the very same Greek words, was the title of the emperor, and this was how the Romans expected him to be venerated. Two rival sons of God, the one man-made, the other appointed by God: it was a dramatic scenario, and indeed a highly charged beginning to Luke's Gospel.

The imperial cult was a very real aspect of life in these parts of the world. Jesus was born under a 'son of God', and he was crucified under another one (Tiberius). By the end of the empire, there had been 182 god-emperors, among literally tens of thousands of lesser deities. More than anything, the imperial cult was the one religion which unified all the tribes, peoples and classes, with one exception: the Jews. Those who did not believe in the One God of the Jews saw the god-emperor as a worldwide, unifying incarnation of their ancient, diverse father-like godheads. In other words, the imperial cult was not just one of many forms of loyalty to the ruler in Rome, and it was far more than a special form of homage. To all intents and purposes, it was a religion, and it functioned like one. Rules were established, they had to be followed if the goodwill of a god was to be secured, and true faith was not expressed by a personal system of belief, but by the meticulous observance of the rules. Piety may have been a part of this system, on an individual basis. A merchant or farmer, for example, who owed his success to the social and political peace established by Augustus may well have had pious feelings of veneration towards the emperor. A Greek inscription found at Olympia explains that 'the divine Augustus exceeded, by his good deeds, even the Olympian gods', and a papyrus found at Oxyrhynchus in Egypt contains a prayer-like invocation of the emperor: 'We swear by Caesar [= Augustus], God, descended from a God'.[3]

Seen from a non-Jewish, non-Christian perspective, such adoration appears understandable – in the province of Asia, for example, well known to readers of the New Testament,[4] the Peace of Augustus, preserved by his successors, lasted until the mid third century, a duration of some three hundred years which has remained unsurpassed in human history. At the same time, no observant Jew could condone this deification. It stood in flagrant contradiction to the First Commandment: 'I am the LORD your God, who brought you out of the land of Egypt, out of the house of slavery; you shall have no other gods before me' (Exodus 20.2). Pious Jews, like those of the Essene community at their centres of Qumran and the south-western hill of Jerusalem, openly condemned this practice, and there is a Qumran text (4Q246) which alludes to Psalm 82.6, a verse in which God judges the usurpers, and where God's wrath is invoked on the Romans with their self-styled god-like emperors.[5] 'The Son of God he will be proclaimed,' we read in this fragment from the Dead Sea Scrolls, 'and the Son of the Most High they will call him. But like the meteors of the vision, so will be their kingdom. They will reign only for a few years on earth, and they will trample all. People will trample people, and one province another province . . . until the people of God will arise and all will rest from the sword.'

Since the imperial cult was not arranged by a central office in Rome, and since the provinces of the empire had different ancestral customs and enjoyed varying levels of autonomy, there were regional differences in its practice. In the Greek-speaking East, provincial benefactors and, in particular, the emperors, were called *Sōtēr*, which means 'Saviour', 'Deliverer'. In her response to the angel's message, Mary calls God her Saviour, and Luke translates her Aramaic with the same Greek word (Luke 1.47). Later, in the story of the Nativity, Jesus himself is called *Sōtēr* (Luke 2.11). And John offers a particularly interesting insight: many Samaritans from Sychar acknowledge Jesus as their Saviour (John 4.42). These Samaritans were the very people who had Herod's temple to the god and saviour Augustus in their city. The term is used in the New Testament more than twenty times, a clear indication of the political and religious awareness of these writers, who recognized the revolution made flesh in the one and only true Saviour, Jesus the Son of God.

In the end, what mattered most to people, not only in the East, was the fact that the emperor had brought peace and that he was the guarantor of eternal peace – he as an individual, and, by virtue of passing on office and status, his successors. Again we recognize a Judaeo-Christian concept: the Messiah (or, in Greek, the Christ) was the bringer of peace. The expectation of a messianic peace permeated Jewish thought, and still does today. In fact, one of the areas where Christians and Jews have always agreed to differ is the definition of this messianic peace. For orthodox Jews, it is primarily a peace on earth which arrives immediately with the Messiah; thus, they find it difficult, if not impossible, to accept the Jew Jesus as the Messiah who has already come. There is no peace on earth, hence on this view Jesus is not the Messiah. It is a very pragmatic, literally 'down to earth' approach, which had its non-Jewish political parallel in the imperial cult: Augustus had brought lasting peace, thus he was the *Sōtēr*, the Saviour. The emperor was truly venerated as a god in the Gentile world, and as we know from inscriptions, occasionally people prayed to him and asked for help in need and illness. In general terms, gods in antiquity all had their different spheres of competence, and the one pertaining to the god-emperor was peace and social well-being. And as far as the emperor's divine popularity was concerned, he had only one rival – outside Judaism and before Christianity became a force to be reckoned with. But this was not some other ruler or god, not one of the many mystery cults, not Mithras, nor Isis and Osiris (which are often quoted as rival forces to the emperor, and also to early Christianity), but a certain Asclepius, known in the Latin West as Aesculapius, the god of healing. Unlike most other gods, but quite like the emperor, he resided on earth (or so we read in texts and inscriptions about him). In other words, if and when he 'healed', his presence could be felt as a real presence. Ascribing a healing to this god was not a merely spiritual idea, it was an experience of the senses. Occasionally, even an emperor like the 'Son of God' Vespasian dabbled in healings.[6]

Emperor gods, philosophers and other healers

Again we realize how Jesus differed from such contemporaries and near-contemporaries. Contrary to the myth perpetuated in some areas of New Testament scholarship, healings and miracle workers were far from common at the time of Jesus. In fact, while Jesus lived, there was only a single – alleged – 'rival', and he lived in Cappadocia: Apollonius of Tyana. All we know about him comes from a single source, the *Life of Apollonius* by Philostratus, who lived in the early third century.[7] Philostratus personifies unreliability. He was an advisor to Julia Domna, who commissioned him to write this 'biography' almost two hundred years after Apollonius' death. Julia, however, was the daughter of a priest of Elgabal, an Arab-Syrian god, and the wife of Emperor Septimius Severus, whom she joined on his expedition to Britain in AD 208–11. Residing at Eboracum (York), Septimius launched several campaigns, and, it seems, initiated the first persecution of Christians in Roman Britain at Verulamium (St Albans), which was carried out by his younger son Geta. According to tradition, the most prominent victim of this persecution was Albanus, St Alban. The sources are contradictory, however, and the anti-Christian attitudes of the Severian family may have been philosophical, rather than physically violent. Christianity, which much like Judaism was often thought of as an unpleasant philosophy rather than a new religion, was fought by 'philosophical' means. And when Julia Domna instructed her courtier Philostratus to write a biography of Apollonius, the ascetic, itinerant neo-Pythagorean preacher and miracle worker who prophesied the deaths of Nero and Domitian and ascended into heaven, that task served precisely that purpose. The message was unambiguous: we, the enlightened Graeco-Romans, can produce such people without needing to have recourse to obscure Galilean Jews. Scholars agree, however, that Philostratus was highly untrustworthy, and the few remaining fragments of writings attributed to Apollonius – a treatise *On Mystical Initiations, or On Sacrifices* and letters which are probably inauthentic – betray a third-rate mind.

His miracles may or may not be pure invention; in any case, they could not have convinced anyone but the most fanatic despiser of Christians that Apollonius was equal, let alone superior, to Jesus of Nazareth. In one instance, the citizens of Ephesus ask him for help against a plague. In front of the theatre, he sees an old, half-blind beggar. He asks the Ephesians to surround him. 'Pick up stones,' he cries, 'as many as you can, and throw them at the enemy of the gods.' The Ephesians hesitate at first – was it not cruel to kill a poor stranger who was crying for pity? But Apollonius insists, and the first stones are thrown. Suddenly, the stranger looks at them with eyes of fire, and the Ephesians recognize the evil spirit. They bury him under stones. After a while, Apollonius orders them to remove the stones, and the man appears to have disappeared. But they see a dog, 'big like a lion, crushed by the stones and with foam at the mouth like rabid animals'.[8] In another miracle, Apollonius resuscitates a bride who had died on her wedding day: he asks for her name and says some words, quietly and inaudibly, into her ear, and she rises from her 'death-like state'.[9] At first glance, there are similarities to the raising of the daughter of Jairus (Mark 5.22–4; 35–43) and of the young man at Nain (Luke 7.11–17), and we may assume that Philostratus had read these Gospels, some 150 years after their first publication. But the ostensible similarities are less remarkable than the decisive difference: Apollonius, the man of mysteries, performs this miracle with inaudible formulas, whereas Jesus speaks clearly and shuns the world of mystic secretiveness.

Philostratus does not hesitate to call Apollonius a god-like man and tells us that others called him a god. We read that Apollonius refuses to be venerated as a god, but Emperor Domitian, himself a son of God (i.e. of Vespasian), asks him, in their fictitious dialogue, why people call him a god, and Apollonius explains that, from their perspective, this is entirely justified.[10]

Philosophers, divine men and emperors were not expected to perform miracles. Among Roman emperors, Vespasian was a first-century exception. Some forty years after the death and resurrection of Jesus, when the Gospels had been written,[11] and when their message was known even in imperial circles,[12] Vespasian healed a man almost blind, and another with a paralysed hand.[13] Vespasian first hesitated; he even mocked those around him. But in order not to look like a coward, he gave in, consulted doctors who analysed both cases as not so severe and advised the emperor to exercise a healing power which, after all, might be in the interest of the gods whose servant he was. Vespasian put spittle on the eyes of the 'blind' man and trod on the hand of the other one, just as they had asked him to do, and they were healed. There is no apparent reason to doubt these two healings. Tacitus, in particular, alerts his readers to the professional quality of his research and, writing in *c.* AD 105, adds a noteworthy comment: 'Eyewitnesses talk about both events to this day, when it would not profit them to tell a lie.' Both cures are known from classical literature; treading on a hand is even recommended in medical treatises.[14]

Neither Apollonius of Tyana nor Vespasian belonged to the Jewish world of Jesus and the first generations of his followers. Within Judaism, the alleged multitude of miracle workers turns out to be a myth invented by New Testament scholarship. We encounter just two Jews credited with miracles in the wider historical context of New Testament times: an earlier one, Honi the Circle-Drawer, who lived in the second/first century BC, and a later one, Hanina ben Dosa, who was active some twenty to thirty years after the death of Jesus. In other words, Hanina does not count, as he came, like Vespasian, too late to influence Jesus and his followers – on the contrary, we may suggest that the stories about Hanina were told in the rabbinical sources, and finally incorporated into the collection of the Babylonian Talmud, to counter the impact of the Jesus message. Hanina's six miracles – over against at least 34 performed by Jesus – are a meagre harvest, anyway, and do not really parallel those of Jesus, either. One of them involves a poisonous snake which bites Hanina's foot; but it is the snake which dies, not Hanina. 'See, my sons,' he explains, 'it is not the snake which kills, but it is sin that kills.' Quite unlike the teachings of Jesus which follow or precede his miracles, Hanina's message is unclear and may even sound ambiguous to the critical mind. Was Hanina more poisonous than the snake, and did he personify the sin which kills?[15] The Gospel parallel occurs in Luke 10.19, where Jesus says: 'See, I have given you authority to tread on snakes and scorpions, and over all the power of the enemy; and nothing will hurt you. Nevertheless, do not rejoice at this, that the spirits submit to you, but rejoice that your names are written in heaven.' The contrast could hardly be starker. Jesus advises humility, and furthermore, the disciples are told to tread on snakes rather than be bitten by them, whereas Hanina, in a far from humble display of his powers, provokes the snake into biting him.[16] Other miracles, such as a 'long-distance healing',[17] may have been modelled on Jesus but do not contribute to a deeper understanding of Hanina as a person, nor of Jewish faith in miracles during the decades after Jesus. And we should not forget that the Talmud may indeed contain early oral traditions, but was finally compiled and completed as late as the reign of Emperor Justinian (AD 527–65), which in the case of Hanina's miracles implies an interval of almost five hundred years.[18] The Gospels, on the other hand, were written and published within decades of the events they describe.

The only other Jewish miracle worker who appears on the scene in the wider context of New Testament times precedes Jesus by up to a century: Honi the Circle-Drawer, a man credited with a single miracle which turns out to be a fine example of Jewish humour. The rainy season was coming to an end, and it had not rained. The people asked Honi to pray for rain. He prayed, but nothing happened. Then he drew a circle, stood in it, and told God that he would not move until God answered his prayers. It began to drizzle. Honi complained. He had not asked for a few drops but for rain that would fill cisterns, pits and caves. The clouds opened, and rain fell with drops as big as barrels. Honi's disciples protested – they feared this rain was going to destroy the world. So Honi explained to God what he really meant: rain of pleasure, rain of blessing, rain of generosity. God complied. Finally, Honi thought that enough was enough and asked God to stop the rain. The grateful people went into the fields to collect truffles and mushrooms.[19] It is obvious enough that Jesus and the first disciples were not emulating this example. Even the later rabbis were divided in their opinions. Some thought that Honi was a great man who encouraged mankind to serve God.[20] Others were puzzled. 'What shall I do with you?' said Rabbi Simeon ben Shetah, one of the leading rabbis at the time of Queen Salome Alexandra. Rabbi Simeon told him bluntly: 'If you were not Honi, I would banish you.' For, as Simeon reasoned, Honi had desecrated 'the name of heaven'. But, he concluded, even though 'you have harassed God with your persistent requests, he has granted you what you wanted, as a father does what his importunate son asks him.' So finally, Rabbi Simeon quoted Proverbs 23.25: 'Let your father and mother be glad; let her who bore you rejoice.' There is not even a shade of a prefiguration of Jesus in such a story.[21]

Jesus was in a league of his own. He 'rivalled' no one, not even the extremely popular Graeco-Roman healing god Asclepius/Aesculapius. And if it is a question of credibility, Jesus wins hands down. Who had ever seen Aesculapius? No one. Who had seen Jesus? Thousands. Who had ever witnessed in person a miracle performed by Aesculapius? No one. Who had seen Jesus performing miracles? Thousands. Did Jesus perform ordinary miracles? No, he did many things that no one – no pagan, no Jew, no emperor, no rabbi – had ever done before. Above all, he accepted, touched and healed the outcasts, the lepers, the untouchables. Not even the later god-emperor Vespasian came anywhere near this breaking of the socio-religious mould.

Jesus redefined all known concepts of divinity alive in the Roman Empire. Those who could not and did not accept his Sonship saw him as a threat to religious and political peace. Caiaphas the high priest certainly did, and so did Pilate, the prefect who represented the emperor. And yet, it was not beyond the world-view of Judaism and the imperial cult to accept Jesus: all his first followers, many thousands of them after all, were Jews, and even Romans acknowledged his divinity early on (cf. Mark 15.39; Acts 10.1–48). Looking at the historical context, we realize how different Jesus really was. The ancient parallels turn out to be a backcloth which merely highlights the revolutionary nature of Jesus the man, and Jesus the Son of God. When Mary passed the temple of Augustus at Sebaste, Gabriel's message on her mind, she, the descendant of Aaron and David, knew that somehow the history of the world was about to change – if God was true to his word.

Locating a divine miracle among the Gentiles

Recent scholarship has shown that the miracles of Jesus are historical. They were accepted as real events even by his most outspoken opponents like the high priest Caiaphas, or, a hundred years later, by the rabid anti-Christian philosopher Celsus.[22] For some of these miracles, sites are mentioned in the Gospels – Cana, Capernaum and Emmaus, for example; for others, the locations remain unknown, as the Gospels do not mention them. And from the perspective of the historian, there is an obvious starting-point: even if certain New Testament scholars assume that most if not all of the miracles are legendary, at least the sites must have existed. If places like Cana, Capernaum or Emmaus never existed, the credibility of the authors would have been less than zero even before the actual story was presented to the readers. One might call this the 'Frederick Forsyth Criterion': the story may be largely fictional, but the telephone booth is exactly where he says it is. Those who read the Gospels in the original Greek will find that practically all the sites are identified by a straightforward place name. On the whole, and whenever the authors saw the need to locate an event, they were at pains to provide details – for example, the detailed description of the pool of Bethesda in John 5.2, or of Peter's house with a forecourt in Capernaum (Mark 1.33), both of which have been confirmed by archaeologists. In some cases, traditions vary and archaeologists have disputed the exact location of certain places and buildings – as in the case of Cana and Emmaus – but even here, patient research has come up with conclusive solutions. There is, however, one notable exception, and it concerns one of the most fascinating and controversial miracles performed by Jesus, a miracle in a pagan, Graeco-Roman environment: the healing of the Gadarene demoniac.

The story as such is well known. Jesus goes east, into pagan territory, to the region of the mainly Greek-speaking cities of the 'Decapolis', a Hellenistic confederation originally of ten cities with tiny Jewish minorities. Gadara, and later Damascus, were its capital cities. With the exception of Bet-Shean (known as Scythopolis in Greek), these cities were east of the River Jordan and the Sea of Galilee. Here, a man 'with an unclean spirit' approaches Jesus. From inside the possessed man, demons converse with him, and Jesus decides to send them into a herd of swine feeding nearby. Some two thousand swine rush down 'the steep bank into the lake' and are drowned. The man is healed and tells the story 'in the city and in the country'. This is how it is told in Mark 5.1–20, Matthew 8.28–34 (where a second man is mentioned) and Luke 8.26–39. Shelves full of exegesis have been produced on the credibility or otherwise of these accounts, on the deeper meaning of the exorcism. Why swine, for example, impure to the Jews, but a very popular source of food for the Gentiles, and why did they have to be drowned in the first place, innocent animals as they may have been? In any case, the Graeco-Roman element is evident. The leading demon addresses Jesus as 'the Son of the Most High God', terminology familiar in the imperial cult (Luke 8.28), combining it, as Luke tells us, with an insight into the superiority of the Jewish God which readers of his Gospel know from 1.32. The demon introduces himself by the name of 'Legion', a term linked with a Roman military presence which has been confirmed locally by archaeologists: a tomb of an officer of the XIVth Legion was discovered in Gadara. Further Roman contingents were stationed near Gerasa. In a figurative sense, 'Legion', then as now, could just mean 'very many people', of course, but it was not a natural term in Greek for that at the time.

However, if we look at modern translations and at the original Greek text, it was not even clear exactly where in the Decapolis the event was supposed to have happened. Or so it seems. In Mark 5.1, the region is called 'the country [or region or territory] of the Gerasenes' (New Revised Standard Version, New International Version, New Jerusalem Bible, etc.), or 'the country of the Gadarenes' (Authorized Version). In Matthew 8.28, it is 'the country [or region or territory] of the Gadarenes' (NRSV, NIV, NJB, etc.), or 'the country of the Gergesenes' (AV). In Luke 8.26, we have 'the country [or region or territory] of the Gerasenes' (NRSV, NIV, NJB, etc.), or 'the country of the Gadarenes' (AV). Clearly, all three Gospel accounts are talking about the same event. But who got it right? Was it Mark, Matthew, or Luke, the modern translations (most of which agree with NRSV, NIV and NJB), or the Authorized Version? Did it happen near the city of Gadara, Gerasa or even Gergesa? Could it perhaps be one of those alleged cases where the Gospel authors themselves did not know what they were talking about?

For all three Gospels, there are ancient manuscripts which offer each of the three place names: Gerasa, Gadara, even Gergesa. But there is not a single ancient codex which has the same name (whichever it may be) in all three. It does not follow, needless to say, that there never was such a codex. But as far as the existing textual evidence is concerned, we can only work with what we have. The oldest surviving papyrus which contains the miracle healing of the demoniac is P75, with Luke's Gospel, dated *c.* AD 150. It has 'Gerasa'. The famous Codex Vaticanus of the fourth century also has this reading. As it happens, the Codex Vaticanus has 'Gerasa' in Mark's Gospel, too. Thus, most modern editions of the Greek text, and most modern translations, prefer 'Gerasa' for both Gospels, and the Authorized Version, whose translators did not yet know these manuscripts, may be excused for preferring 'Gadara'. But if the moderns are happy with 'Gerasa' in Mark and Luke, why does it have to be 'Gadara' in Matthew? The very same Codex Vaticanus which offers us 'Gerasa' in Mark and Luke has 'Gadara' in Matthew. To complicate matters further, another important codex, the Alexandrinus at the British Library in London, of the fifth century, has 'Gadara' in Mark and Luke and a gap where the passage in Matthew would have been. Was the Alexandrinus perhaps the one codex where all the Gospels read 'Gadara'? Obviously, we cannot tell. And yet it is absurd to assume, as do the editors of the current Greek text, that the Gospel authors placed the same event at two different sites.[23] There is also no text-critical or exegetical reason to assume that these authors pieced together different stories with different locations. If the manuscript tradition does not provide an unambiguous solution, it is simply one of those instances which are very common in pagan classical literature, but extremely rare in the New Testament, where the manuscript evidence appears to be inconclusive. So what does the classical scholar do next? He or she investigates the geography and the archaeological data. In other words, which site near the eastern shore of the Sea of Galilee agrees with the information provided by the story?

We immediately find a striking argument against Gerasa. This city, the modern Jerash, is some fifty kilometres south-south-east of the lake and did not reach as far as the lake in any of its parts. On the other hand Gadara, today's Um Qeia, is a mere eight kilometres south-east of the lake and did have territory adjacent to the lake.[24] It even had its own harbour, recently re-excavated at a place called Tell Samra. Furthermore, coins from Gadara show boats and emphasize the link with the Sea of Galilee.[25] Thus, the historical and topographical solution is straightforward enough: Gerasa must be excluded, and Gadara is the answer. If this is so simple, how could 'Gerasa' creep into ancient manuscripts and influence even present-day translations of Mark and Luke? First of all, it is plausible to assume a misspelling which was copied and re-copied. It was easy enough to confuse Gadara with Gerasa, particularly at a time when copyists no longer knew the actual geography of the Holy Land. And what is more, at the period of the most influential Christian codices, Gerasa was still an important cultural centre with a temple dedicated to Zeus and a theatre, and it had become the seat of a bishop under Emperor Constantine. Gadara, on the other hand, had lost its earlier fame as the home town of once famous authors like Menippus, Meleager and Philodemus. At the time of Jesus, Gadara still revelled in this cultural glory, but when the influential codices were written and copied, Gadara was largely forgotten, whereas Gerasa continued to thrive. In other words, the involuntary or perhaps even conscious substitution of 'Gerasa' for 'Gadara' was an understandable error of fourth-century scribes.

But if we now look at the actual accounts again, there is a striking detail which does favour Gadara, even apart from the fact that Gerasa did not have access to the lake, whereas Gadara did: the swineherds 'ran off and told it in the city' (Mark 5.14). All the stories agree that this city was near the place where the miracle had happened. It is obvious that eight kilometres – about one hour, or less, at running pace – is what the accounts imply, rather than the fifty kilometres in the case of Gerasa, a journey involving an overnight stop. Furthermore, Mark 4.35 informs us that Jesus and the disciples intended to 'go across to the other side', and Gadara and its harbour, on the south-eastern shore, are diagonally opposite north-western Capernaum. What remains to be accounted for is an oddity of the tradition which led to a tourist site frequented by Christian pilgrims even today, Kursi on the north-eastern shore of the Sea of Galilee. It is the 'Gergesa' which we encounter in the Authorized Version of Matthew's Gospel. This mistake is due to Origen, the famous librarian and theologian at Caesarea Maritima (*c.* AD 185–254). He correctly decided that Gerasa must be excluded because it was too far away. But in his day, Gadara was of no importance, and even the fact that it once had a harbour was unknown. Thus, he began to look for a third site. And he 'found' it opposite Capernaum, where steep cliffs formed a precipice: the ideal location, or so he thought, for a herd of swine to fall into the lake. He called the place 'Gergesa', without any previous evidence for this name, and even invented his own etymology: 'Gergesa' allegedly means 'the habitation of those who drove away', i.e. of those who drove away the Lord by asking him to leave them after the miracle.[26] This, in itself, is quite ingenious, since the three Gospel accounts do tell us that the people did not want Jesus to stay, probably because they were afraid of losing their livelihood should Jesus decide to drive even more herds with thousands of swine into the lake. But

Origen was too clever by half. The etymology does not work, and a place called Gergesa never existed. However, Origen was probably the most influential Christian scholar of his time, and thus his 'solution' crept into a number of late copies of the Gospels, among them the mid-fourth-century Codex Sinaiticus, the oldest of the codices of the whole Bible in Greek, where it is the original reading in Luke, and an 'amended' reading in Matthew and Mark.[27]

The situation was complicated further by another great man of the early Church, Jerome (*c.* 350–420), who mistakenly believed the site of the miracle to be Chorazin, north of the lake and three kilometres from Capernaum. In the sixth century its name became 'Chorsia', which in Arabic was turned into 'Kursiya' ('chair', 'throne') and finally into the modern name of the tourist site, Kursi. Here the early Byzantine Church built memorial chapels and churches; their impressive fifth-/sixth-century ruins have been excavated. Curiously though, some scholars, keen to defend the even more obscure traditions of the early Church, have supported the Byzantine 'Gergesa'.[28] There is nothing but one far-fetched textual argument in their favour. In our modern translations, we read in Joshua 3.10, 'Joshua said: "By this you shall know that among you is the living God who without fail will drive out from before you the Canaanites, Hittites, Hivites, Perizzites, Girgashites, Amorites, and Jebusites."' But in the Septuagint version of this verse, the Girgashites have become the 'Gergesaioi'. In the Codex Vaticanus, a variant reading of Joshua 12.5 even turns the Geshurites into 'Gergesei'. No one knows where these people may have lived. If Origen found the 'Gergesans' in his Greek scroll of Joshua 3.10, it may have inspired him to place them in the region of what, in his days, had become the Decapolis. The variant of Joshua 12.5 in the Codex Vaticanus is of no use, as it is some one hundred years later than Origen.[29] But all these efforts to rescue Origen and later Byzantine tradition remain wild speculation. For the specialists, they are an entertaining exercise in the study of knowledge lost and traditions invented. Having rejected Gerasa, and unaware of the solid evidence in favour of Gadara, Christians in the third, fourth and fifth centuries created a new site and lived with it happily ever after.

Theologically speaking, there is nothing wrong with a visit to Kursi. It remains a beautiful spot, where it is as convenient to remember a miracle of Jesus as it is uplifting to sit in the compound of the quiet, prayerful 'Garden Tomb' in Jerusalem – which must be ruled out, for archaeological reasons, as the historical site of Jesus' burial and resurrection, but which just feels so much more authentic than the unattractive nineteenth-century kiosk which covers the actual site in the Church of the Holy Sepulchre. The true site of the miracle of the demoniac and the swine, somewhere near Gadara's harbour on the south-eastern shore of the lake, is not yet accessible to visitors; even the ancient port has not been properly excavated. But at least we know that this is the area presupposed by all three Gospels. Anyone driving north from Bet-Shean and turning right towards Kibbutz En Gev, rather than left towards Tiberias, will pass it. For editors and translators of the New Testament, the next step will be to use 'Gadara' in all three Gospel versions.

And for those interested in historical backgrounds, it may be of interest to point out that at Gadara, Jesus performed a miracle which targeted non-Jews, the Hellenized people of the eastern Decapolis, using swine, which were impure and untouchable to the Jews, but an everyday commodity and certainly of less value than humans and their well-being in the eyes of the pagans. At the time of Jesus and the first readers of the Gospels, when all of the manuscripts must have read 'Gadara', the country of the Gadarenes epitomized Graeco-Roman culture, philosophy and poetry, with some of the most popular writers of Hellenistic literature. In fact, the continuous popularity of Gadarene authors like the above-mentioned Menippus and Meleager, and the rediscovery of some one thousand scrolls with the writings of Philodemus in the 'Villa dei Pisoni' in Herculaneum – before AD 79, when Herculaneum was covered under the ash of the eruption of Vesuvius – can be understood as evidence of the far-reaching impact of Gadara in New Testament times. Even in the late first and early second century, when the first scrolls and codices of the Gospels had reached non-Christian readers, Gadara remained a source of Greek philosophy: Oenomaus, a cynic who may have been of Jewish origin, lived there at the time. Eusebius, the fourth-century church historian, quoted him at length and used some of his tenets in arguments against paganism.

The ministry of Jesus was inclusive: it was meant for Jews and non-Jews alike. As for the Gospel accounts of the Gadarene miracle, the quest for the authentic site reminds us of this essential fact of his eternal message.

The beginning as summary: Mark's first sentence

World literature does not offer many examples of a first sentence which sums up the essential, previously unheard of, provocative message of the whole text. Mark's Gospel is such a case, and it broadens the cross-cultural ground covered in this chapter. It is no secret among classical philologists: Mark's Gospel is one of the greatest works of Hellenistic literature. Far from being a hastily concocted, unhistorical, amateurish effort in awful Greek, it is a brilliant study written by a master of Greek sentence structure and grammar. His skill is evident from the very first sentence – a perfect introduction: 'The beginning of the gospel of Jesus Christ, the Son of God'. To us, it looks almost too obvious. Of course a work begins with the beginning, so why say so? From our point of view after almost two thousand years, it is simply a Gospel, telling us about Jesus, that Jesus is the Christ, and, as we proclaim often enough in the creeds, that he is the Son of God. In other words, Mark's introductory sentence does not seem remarkable. But if we read it from the perspective of a first-century readership, we realize that every word is charged with previously unknown, tantalizing, revolutionary meaning. Let us take a closer look.

Mark's first word, in Greek, is *arche*, beginning. To a Jew, this was an allusion to the first Hebrew word of the Bible, *bereshit*: the very beginning, when God created the world (Genesis 1.1). The Septuagint has *en archē*: 'In the beginning God created'. Readers of the New Testament find a precise echo in the first words of John's Gospel: 'In the beginning [*en archē*] was the word'. Mark's Gospel, however, was not written exclusively for Jews and Jewish Christians. It also targeted a wider pagan readership, in Rome, where it was written, and elsewhere in the Roman Empire.[30] And for those readers, *archē* carried a different connotation: it reminded them of Greek philosophy. From the sixth century BC, in a thinker like Anaximander, it signified the fundamental, original laws which controlled the world.[31] Plato (427–347 BC) linked the concept of an imperishable *archē* with the immortality of the soul.[32] And in Aristotle's *Poetics*, the great fourth-century Greek philosopher (384–322 BC) established the use of the word 'beginning', *archē*, as a technical term, to indicate the beginning of new dramatic action.[33] Mark subtly reaches both of his target groups: those with a Jewish background by reminding them of the presence of a creator God, and those from a pagan background by alluding to a concept of immortality and high drama, conceived by two of the greatest thinkers of Greek antiquity. In fact, many Jews, particularly in the Diaspora, were themselves educated in Greek literature and philosophy. For them, Mark's first word could function as a twofold invitation. It was as though the author was playing on a harpsichord with two manuals, doubling the impact of his composition.

The second and third Greek words in Mark's introductory sentence, *tou euangeliou*, 'of the gospel', are even more fascinating. Before this first of the Gospels to be published became widely known, the term was of course unknown in its Christian meaning. The Greek word as such, however, was quite common. Literally every citizen of the Roman Empire would have recognized it: *euangelia*, 'good news', were the birthdays of the emperor and the anniversaries of his accession to power. This inscription, found at Priene in Asia Minor and dated to the year 9 BC, is one of many which have survived: 'Anniversary of the god Augustus, beginning of the good news for the whole world which was announced by him.' Readers of classical literature would also have remembered the word from Homer's epic *Odyssey*, where it means the reward for the messenger who brings the good news.[34] And Mark's Jewish readership? They would have encountered it in the Septuagint. The Septuagint has different names and numbers for some of the Old Testament books, so the Greek references have to be translated into our terminology. Thus, we find the word four times in the Septuagint's 2 Kings (which, in our Bibles, is 2 Samuel): 18.20, 22, 25, 27, and once in 4 Kings (2 Kings in our Bibles), 7.9. Each time, it is used in the plural. Only once is the singular used, in 2 Kings (i.e. 2 Samuel) 4.10. It simply means 'good news', without any prophetic or messianic overtones. Those of Mark's readers in Rome and elsewhere who had read the Latin classics would have recognized the terminology of the great orator and philosopher Cicero (106–43 BC). In his letters to his friend, the wealthy editor and bookseller Titus Pomponius Atticus, he employs the Greek word in the middle of the Latin text. 'First, the – as I think – *euangelia*', he writes.[35]

Again, it becomes apparent that Mark appeals equally to his Jewish as well as to his pagan readership. Homer, Aristotle, Cicero, the cult of the emperor, 2 Samuel and 2 Kings: wherever one looked, a world of expectation was linked to the *euangelia*, the good news. Mark's interpretive virtuosity does not end here, however. Alone among the ancients (Homer apart, where the term refers to the reward, not to the actual news), he uses 'good news' in the singular. Attentive readers would have noticed it straight away; for others, it would become apparent in the course of the text: in his book, the panoply of good news was abolished. In place of the multitude of good news, there now was only one, in the singular: the one and only *euangelion*. But whose was it? An unknown emperor's perhaps? The answer follows in the next word of Mark's first sentence: 'Jesus'.

A first-century reader would have been puzzled. In the Jewish world, it was the third most common name. Jesus who? Even in the New Testament, we encounter several people called Jesus: Jesus Barabbas (Matthew 27.16), Jesus Bar Eliezer (Luke 3.29), Jesus Justus (Colossians 4.11). They are all identified by a reference to their father or to a byname. The same applies, of course, to the Jesus everyone immediately associates with the name – he is not just Jesus, but Jesus of Nazareth or Jesus the Nazorean. Even Pontius Pilate made sure everyone understood who he was crucifying. On the headboard attached to the cross, the Passover pilgrims from all over the Jewish world read in Hebrew, Greek and Latin that he was Jesus of Nazareth (John 19.19).[36] Throughout the Roman Empire, 'Jesus' was a name associated with immigrant Jews, mainly from the lower classes, servants and slaves among them. Imagine the surprise for non-Jewish readers. Historical biographies dealt with well-known heroes, with emperors, high-ranking civil servants, procurators – but never with unknown people of obscure origin from outside the Graeco-Roman nobility. In other words, those readers were both shocked and curious. How could any author dare to write about such a person? What on earth makes him worthy of *euangelia*? Why is there a dramatic new beginning associated with this man? The next word, or so they hoped, would provide the clue. And this next word is *Christos*, Christ.

Again, we know (or think we know) exactly what the word means: Christ, in Hebrew 'Messiah', is the Anointed One of God. In the New Testament, it is a title always used to define Jesus: 'Jesus the Christ', Paul calls him, or 'the Christ Jesus'. However, it is not a second personal name, as many Christians think today, but a Jewish title derived from the Old Testament. In the Septuagint, *Christos* occurs several times, in different contexts. In Leviticus 4.5, for example, it describes the anointed priest. In the Greek text of 1 Kings (= 1 Samuel) 24.7, David refuses to kill Saul, because Saul the king is 'the anointed of the Lord', the *christos kyriou*, or, literally, 'the Christ of the LORD'. In Psalm 18.50 and elsewhere in the Psalms, it is clearly messianic and signifies the Anointed One of God. But it was also used for a non-Jew, the Persian king Cyrus, as a saviour of the Jews: 'Thus says the Lord to his anointed, to Cyrus, whose right hand I have grasped to subdue the nations before him,' we read in Isaiah 45.1; and 'anointed' here is *christos*. On the other hand, people who did not know the Jewish scriptures and therefore did not see anything sacred in the term were perplexed. *Christos*, in plain Greek, was something 'to be rubbed on', to be 'used as an ointment or salve'. Was this Jesus in the first verse of Mark's Gospel a sick man? Or was he an athlete, a prospective winner at the next Olympic Games, about to be massaged with oils? To a Graeco-Roman readership, it was quite mysterious. At this stage, though, they understood that the author was not dabbling in myths and legends. An unknown Jesus, sick or about to be made fit for competition, a man whose *euangelia* were announced, was firmly rooted in real life. He belonged to the socio-political world of the times – the terminology was unmistakable. But who was he? A rival to the Roman emperor who originated from the East, where athletes often had tens of thousands of devoted followers? The next two words must bring the solution, those readers would have thought. And indeed, they did.

'Son of God', *Huios Theou*, we read. As we saw above, Jewish readers may have recognized the description from the writings of Philo of Alexandria, the great Jewish philosopher who died *c.* AD 50. He called Abraham a 'son of God'.[37] In the Old Testament, the idea that a successor of David's will be God's son is first expressed in 2 Samuel 7.14 (in the Greek Bible, 2 Kings 7.14), where it says: 'I will be to him a father, and he shall be to me a son'. And so we could go on. Whether or not the Jewish writers of these books envisaged a son of God conceived by God the Holy Spirit, God's only-begotten Son, as we proclaim him in the creeds, is of no concern at this point. Every Jew would, at the very least, see the term in the context of God acting among men. For Graeco-Roman readers, the answer was even more unambiguous. They all knew who the son of God was, from inscriptions, coins and papyri: the son of God was the Roman emperor. Ever since Augustus had persuaded the Senate to style his adoptive father 'the divine one' (*Divus*),

51

the son of such an elevated ruler was 'the son of the divine one', the *filius Divi*. In the Greek-speaking parts of the empire, 'divine' and 'God' were the same word, so the son of the divine one became the son of God, the *Huios Theou*. And remember that Jesus was born under a son of God, Augustus, and crucified under a son of God, Tiberius.

Greek and Roman readers who saw the words 'Son of God' at the end of Mark's first sentence had no choice: they had to think of the Roman emperor. And it was not just a polite formula. As we saw at the beginning of this chapter, the imperial cult was a serious matter, particularly in the East – there were 37 temples dedicated to Augustus while he was still alive, and 19 more after his death. Thus, those readers of Mark's Gospel would have understood that the new dramatic beginning, the hitherto unheard-of good news, did indeed concern a rival to the emperors. The unknown Jewish Jesus with his ointment was a force to be reckoned with. Not a myth, not a legend, but a religious and political challenge to the established system.

It goes without saying that those first readers would have felt compelled to find out more. Mark's introduction, one of the most brilliant beginnings in Greek literature, would have transfixed Jewish and non-Jewish readers alike. And let us finally remember Mark's subtlety in the middle of the sentence. Accustomed to the plural of the good news, the *euangelia*, those readers now find that Mark employs the singular, *euangelion*. With Jesus the Christ, the true and only Son of God (1 John 4.9), the one and only piece of good news that matters to mankind has been proclaimed. It is, indeed, a singular message of salvation.

4 Crossing Borders: Jesus in Galilee and Syrophoenicia, and at the Shrine of Pan

> Quite a lot of questions, thought his lordship, and some of them
> unanswerable till outside reports came in.
>
> Dorothy L. Sayers, *The Nine Tailors*

> For just as it is harmful to drink wine alone, or, again, to drink
> water alone, while wine mixed with water is sweet and delicious
> and enhances one's enjoyment, so also the style of the story delights
> the ears of those who read the work.
>
> 2 Maccabees 15.39

Listening, observing, communicating

The ministry of Jesus was a very public one. Even on those occasions
when he taught three or four of his disciples in private (the three being
Peter, James and John, who were sometimes joined by Peter's brother
Andrew), his teaching was ultimately passed on to others. And when
the Gospels were 'published', these intimate conversations became
general knowledge. Those who could not read or did not have their
own scrolls of the Gospels would not have been excluded. Texts were
read aloud, at meetings or in small circles, and any interested passer-
by could hear what a person was reading – in those days, 'silent
libraries' were unknown, as people normally read their scrolls out
loud. Thus, in the passage quoted from 2 Maccabees above, it really
is the ears of those who read the work which are delighted, and not the
eyes. When Philip meets the treasurer of the Nubian Queen Mother,
the Candace, on the road to Gaza and asks him, 'Do you understand
what you are reading?' (Acts 8.30), it is obvious that the man up in his
carriage was reading from a scroll of Isaiah loudly enough for Philip
to identify the text. In other words, the literary traditions of early
Christianity were almost automatically and simultaneously oral traditions as well. Conversely, details passed on by word of mouth were
not just memorized. Most people assume that the stories about Jesus,

and his sayings, were left purely to oral traditions for many decades before the first author set pen to paper. From the historian's perspective, the alternative view is equally valid: local communities and individuals recorded sayings of Jesus, the wandering preacher, on broken pieces of pottery, the so-called *ostraca* – one of the most important sources of information from antiquity in general – or on scraps of papyrus, passed them on to others who read them to those who were willing to listen, who in turn memorized them and thus distributed the message by word of mouth. This way, even the completed Gospels, all of them written during the eyewitness period, would have inspired further oral traditions.[1] We should bear this in mind if we want to understand how some of the seemingly 'secret' teachings, and the apparently exclusive 'outside reports', contribute to the mosaic of the multifaceted, international world of Jesus.

It is no accident that the very first Christians, including the authors of the New Testament writings, were Jews.[2] Their intimate knowledge of their own traditions was grudgingly admired by the decidedly anti-Jewish Roman philosopher Seneca (*c.* AD 4–65): 'They [the Jews], admittedly, know the reasons for their customs; the greater part of our people does what it does without knowing why.'[3] Reading, writing and memorizing were an integral part of Jewish upbringing, and the synagogues formed the nucleus of this system. Archaeological evidence provides a clue. On Masada, the fortress of nationalistic Jews in their last stand against the Romans, the school and the synagogue itself were kept active even during the desperate final years, until the conquest in AD 73/4.[4] In a male-orientated society, women did not have automatic access to primary schools and other forms of education in and around the synagogues. But even if we admit that the writing, copying and dissemination of literature was a male prerogative in classical antiquity (including Jewish and Jewish-Christian society), we should nevertheless be willing to accept that this 'one-sided' educational system was, as such, efficient enough to guarantee a standard of upbringing which was the envy of the Romans. This was an important factor at the time of Jesus and his contemporaries, and we need to stay aware of its influence at the time. We are not talking about uneducated builders, peasants and fishermen. Jesus and his disciples acted in a multilingual and cosmopolitan environment, not as strangers, but as well-informed Jews who 'knew the ropes'.

The northern territories of Galilee, the Decapolis in the East, and the tetrarchy of Philip, with Caesarea Philippi as its capital, attracted people from all over the eastern provinces of the Roman Empire. Travelling with Jesus and his first followers, we can easily see how the crossing of borders into these regions enriched the depth and width of his message, and how it appealed to audiences from different backgrounds. For most of his Galilean ministry, Jesus' home base was Simon Peter's house in Capernaum. Matthew calls it 'his own town' (Matthew 9.1; Mark 2.1). Capernaum, or in Hebrew 'kephar nakhûm', the village of Nahum, was an important fishing port not far from the border between the tetrarchy of Herod the Great's son Philip and the Galilean territory of another son, Herod Antipas. Thus, there was a customs office (Mark 2.14; Matthew 9.9) and a Roman garrison (Matthew 8.5–13, Luke 7.1–10). The extensive moorings, where the customs office was situated, and the garrison with its baths, north-east of the town but within walking distance (Luke 7.6), have been excavated. Archaeologists have uncovered extensive docks, 700 metres long.[5] The production of olive oil, the cultivation of grain, and glasswork were further sources of income. The famous Via Maris, passing nearby, guaranteed easy access to international trade.[6] With an estimated 1,500 inhabitants, Capernaum was small, but certainly not poor. Main roads, wide enough for vehicles, separated blocks of houses built in solid basalt, three metres high, with inner courtyards, and outside staircases leading to a clay roof (see Luke 5.18–19). The fishing companies of Zebedee and sons (James and John), and Simon Peter and Andrew, owned several boats for different types of fishing: dragnet boats, as in Matthew 13.47–8 and John 21.8–11, others where the nets were pulled in (Luke 5.6–7), and smaller ones for just two people fishing near the shore (Mark 1.18). On one occasion, several of these boats and their crews put to sea: 'They took him with them in the boat, just as he was, and there were other boats with him' (Mark 4.36).[7]

The Roman garrison itself was another source of regular income. Fish, oil, and cereal products were sold to the canteen. We do not know how large and wealthy the contingent stationed at Capernaum was in those days, but one of the commanding officers, a centurion, was rich enough to sponsor the construction of the synagogue (Luke 7.5). There is no reason to doubt the Gospel account. Covering an area of 20 by 8 metres, it was much smaller than the fifth-century building whose restored remains can be seen today, and more comparable in size to the synagogue at Magdala (Migdal) further south. And non-Jews did indeed fund synagogues, whether because they were attracted to Judaism, or because they wanted to further good relations with their neighbours.[8] In any case, such a pro-Jewish Roman would have been in frequent contact with the Jewish community. He learned from them, and they, in turn, learned from him. Greek rather than Latin was the common language of soldiers and officers in the East, and if they read Jewish literature – as the centurion at Capernaum may well have done – it would have been the Greek version of the Old Testament, the Septuagint. Getting on with the Romans meant speaking Greek (with a smattering of Latin). But the Jews in this region knew Greek anyway, and they needed it, like those in Nazareth, Sepphoris and other parts of Galilee near international trading routes, for their daily business. Capernaum, in other words, was a place where people met: traders, soldiers and their commanders, and well-to-do fishing entrepreneurs. Jesus was aware of all this when he set up house in Capernaum. The village was small enough for him to be noticed, and it was central enough, like his family home at Nazareth, to access the world that mattered.

Capernaum offered another strategic advantage which Nazareth did not have: it was a border town, within walking distance of mainly non-Jewish, Hellenistic territories. To the east, the Gaulanitis (hence the modern name 'Golan') began after some eight kilometres; 25 kilometres to the north, and to the west of Lake Semechonitis (today's Hule Nature Reserve), there were the eastern regions of the territory of Tyre and Sidon in Syrophoenicia. Jesus made use of these geopolitical opportunities on more than one occasion. His activities were not always as dramatic as the exorcism near the harbour of Gadara in the Decapolis, but they certainly reveal a fact which has been disputed by some New Testament scholars for a long time: Jesus did indeed involve non-Jews in his proclamation of the Kingdom of God from the very beginning.

The Roman centurion's servant whom Jesus healed at Capernaum (Luke 7.1–10) may have been a Jewish civilian employee, but the centurion himself, who accepted the authority of Jesus, was a representative of the imperial power. Another early incident occurs when Jesus leaves Capernaum to go 'to the region of Tyre' (Mark 7.24) in Syrophoenicia. A woman approaches him, and Mark describes her as 'Greek-speaking'[9] (7.26). She asks him to heal her daughter and receives a curious answer: 'Let the children be fed first, for it is not fair to take the children's food and throw it to the dogs.' 'Lord, even the dogs under the table eat the children's crumbs,' she replies, and Jesus fulfils her request: 'For saying that, you may go – the demon has left your daughter' (Mark 7.27–9). The woman knew what Jesus was implying and replied accordingly: the children are the Jews. For Gospel readers who may not have understood this metaphor, Matthew spells it out in his version of the event: 'I was sent only to the lost sheep of the house of Israel' (Matthew 15.24). However, Matthew, like Mark, knew that there must have been more to this statement than a negative expression of rejection. He had told the story of the Gentile centurion in 8.5–13 and reported Jesus' commendation: 'Truly I tell you, in no one in Israel have I found such faith' (8.10). Thus, Matthew's expansion of Mark's account, where we read 'first' instead of 'only', should not be interpreted as a statement of policy. Having tested the woman's determination (and devout quick-wittedness), he gives in immediately. Jesus never performed a miracle unless he knew that the recipient believed in his powers. In this respect, he did not distinguish between Jews and Gentiles. The healing of the Syrophoenician woman's daughter was no turning point; it confirmed an open-mindedness which had always been there. We should not forget that it was Jesus who had taken the decision to go into Syrophoenician territory in the first place, and who obviously was quite capable of conducting a conversation in Greek.

When – as told in Mark 8.13–21 and Matthew 15.32–9 – Jesus feeds a multitude of people for the second time, the new incident is located on the eastern shores of the lake, in the Gaulanitis, and a simple linguistic detail tells us that the people he fed came from a Greek, Hellenistic background. After the first feeding, that of the five thousand, the remaining pieces of fish and bread were collected in baskets which Mark and Matthew call *kophinos*. They were the typical shopping baskets of the Jews, so characteristic in fact that the Roman satirist Juvenal (*c.* AD 60–130) later describes the Jews by referring to this basket: 'Here [at the Porta Capena], where Numa had his meetings with his nightly mistress, the holy fount and grove are let out to Jews, whose goods are a *cophinus* and hay.'[10] And in another satire he writes about 'a trembling Jewess, leaving her *cophinus* with hay behind, comes begging'.[11] But when Jesus feeds 'the four thousand men, besides women and children', the remnants are collected in baskets called *spyris* in

Greek, and this is the typical technical term for shopping baskets in the Hellenistic world. This second feeding, for the Greek-speaking Gentiles, may be seen as a sequel to the incident in the region of Tyre – Jesus accepts that non-Jews need his attention now, not later, and he provides it unhesitatingly. To see it like this would be an over-simplification, however. The Gadara exorcism, told in Mark 5, took place before the meeting with the Syrophoenician woman, and we should conclude that Jesus was never opposed to a ministry among the non-Jewish population. All of this is summed up in the climax of his northern teachings and miracles: the walk from Bethsaida to Caesarea Philippi and Peter's proclamation of Jesus as Messiah and God's Son in front of a shrine of the pagan god Pan and a temple of Emperor Augustus. Let us start in Bethsaida.

Follow the cowpats

'Follow the cowpats!' This was good advice, freely given to historians and archaeologists looking for remains of ancient Bethsaida, not far from the northern edge of the Sea of Galilee. A Benedictine archaeologist at the Abbey of the Dormition (Hagio Maria Sion) in Jerusalem, the late Bargil Pixner, was the first to suggest that the Bethsaida of the Gospels should be found on 'Et Tel', where the Syrians had dug in during the Yom Kippur War, leaving behind ammunition boxes, hand grenades and mines all over the area when they fled. However, where cows had stood and left their pats without being blown up, it was safe for archaeologists to walk – and this was how Pixner and his colleagues began to dig at one of the controversial sites of biblical archaeology. Today, visitors no longer need to negotiate the mines left by the Syrian forces in Bethsaida, as it has become an archaeological park open to tourists. But they now need to negotiate its very own minefield of scholarly controversy.

Pixner's starting point was obvious to all historically trained readers of ancient texts: there undoubtedly was a settlement called Bethsaida. The Gospels mention it as the place of origin of three disciples, Peter, Andrew and Philip (John 1.44, 12.21), and as the place where Jesus healed a blind man (Mark 8.22–6). It is the starting point of the journey to Caesarea Philippi, where Jesus was proclaimed Messiah by Peter (Mark 8.22 with 27), and it is one of the towns cursed by Jesus (Luke

10.13). Besides the Gospels, the Roman admiral and encyclopaedist Pliny the Elder and the Jewish historian Flavius Josephus also refer to Bethsaida. As commander of the Jewish revolutionaries, Josephus had fought near Bethsaida in a battle against the Romans, in AD 66.[12] The east–west axis to Akko (ancient Ptolemais, Acts 21.7) and Tyre, or, in the other direction, into the Decapolis, was equally important and had been used by Jesus (Mark 7.24–39). In 3 BC, at about the time when Peter, Andrew and Philip were born, the Tetrarch Philip, one of the sons of Herod the Great, had elevated the town to the status of a city. He loved it so much that he wanted to be buried there, rather than in his capital, Caesarea Philippi.[13] In AD 30, four years before he died, Philip named it 'Julias', in honour of Julia, the wife of Emperor Augustus and mother of the future Emperor Tiberius, on the first anniversary of her death.[14] Thus, Bethsaida must have existed. But where was it?

Imagine an archaeologist who opts for a fishing town (or city) several miles from the seashore. It sounds like a mad idea. But this is precisely what Pixner did when he published his first article about the site in 1982.[15] After some initial ridicule, his Israeli colleagues carried out a number of surveys, excavations began two years later, and in 1989, his Bethsaida was officially acknowledged by the Israel Antiquities Authority as the site mentioned by Josephus. At Bethsaida, archaeological research, mainly conducted by Rami Arav and Fred Strickert, has established the likelihood of a surprising scenario: there was more than one Bethsaida. There were two, but they belonged together: first, the 45,000 square metres of the city on the hill, not as far away from the shore as it seems today, since the ancient shoreline was further north; and second, a suburb, at the edge of the lake. Fishermen lived in both the city on the hill (houses with fishing equipment have been found) and down by the sea. Due to a quirk of Herodian heritage, the coastline, with the lower settlement, was in the territory of Herod Antipas. To most people at the time, however, the upper town and the lower part, with the fishing harbour, both belonged to the same settlement. In any case, John the Evangelist clearly calls lower Bethsaida a 'city' (in Greek, a *polis*: John 1.44). But while the border did not interfere with daily life, it may have influenced later developments. For by Byzantine times, the former tetrarchy of Philip had long since lost its status and importance, whereas the settlements along the shore of the lake continued to flourish. In the early second century, a disastrous earthquake destroyed upper Bethsaida.

Byzantine Christian pilgrims had to make do with what they saw, and settled for the lower Bethsaida. A magnificent church was built, and Willibald of Wessex, later Bishop of Eichstaett in south-east Germany, saw and described it in the mid-seventh century.[16] The ruins there, with their Arabic name Hirbet El Aradsh, are still impressive and await further excavation once the ongoing work on the hill, two kilometres away, has been concluded.

The discovery of a wine jar in a cellar of Et Tel on the hill gave particular pleasure to Bargil Pixner. The surviving fragment of pottery showed an incised cross with arms of equal length, and with beams emanating from the centre, reminiscent of a symbol used in the worship of gods like the Romano-Syrian 'Sol Indiges', a sun god. But at a later stage, someone had extended the vertical bar downwards to form a Christian cross. Pixner and others assumed that this wine jar was used by Jewish Christians at Bethsaida for the celebration of Holy Communion, and that the symbol of a sun god was easily Christianized in view of Psalm 84.12 or Luke 1.78, where God and Christ are compared to the sun. Since the destructive earthquake at Bethsaida took place on the night of 13 December AD 115, this potsherd must be older. It convinced Pixner, and many scholars who have studied the evidence, of the very early pictorial origins of the cross as the definitive Christian symbol. On the basis of texts like Matthew 16.24 and 1 Corinthians 1.18, it was turned from a symbol of shame – in the eyes of non-Christian Jews and Romans – into a symbol of triumph for all followers of Christ, centuries before it became part of official Christian art, theology and politics.[17]

From Bethsaida to Caesarea

The ancient road from Bethsaida to Caesarea can still be traced across the landscape. With the possible exception of a stopover in Bethsaida below the hill, Jesus and the disciples would have walked entirely on territory belonging to Philip the Tetrarch, in the Gaulanitis. The Gaulanitis reached from Mount Hermon in the north to the River Yarmuk in the south-east – stretching some seventy kilometres; to the west, the River Jordan was its natural border. The southern parts were populated by Jews and non-Jews alike, although in and around the bigger towns and villages, and especially between Bethsaida and the capital Caesarea, Jews were in the minority, and Greek was the predominant language. Philip himself may have been the driving force behind this increasing 'Hellenization' during the lifetime of Jesus. Like two of his stepbrothers, he had studied in Rome.[18] After his father's death, Emperor Augustus gave him the Gaulanitis, adding the Batanaea (to the east), Trachonitis (to the north-east), Hauranitis (to the south of the Batanaea) and parts of Ituraea (to the west of the district of Paneas, which Philip renamed 'Caesarea', to honour Caesar Augustus). This vast territory secured him an annual income of 100 talents.[19] This is no precise amount, as a 'talent' was a weight rather than a definitive amount of money, but most scholars translate it as 600,000 denarii or drachmas. It is always difficult to convert such amounts into modern currencies, but it has been suggested that one denarius equals roughly £140 today. In other words, Philip's regular income was huge enough for him to invest in the rebuilding and exten-sion of cities in Graeco-Roman style, from Bethsaida to Paneas/ Caesarea. Since he did not have to worry about offending the religious sensibilities of the few Jews in his tetrarchy, he minted coins with images, mainly of the two successive emperors under whom he served, Augustus and Tiberius. Some coins show a temple – not the one in Jerusalem, but probably the temple of Augustus and Roma which his father had had built at Paneas. The references in the New Testament (Luke 3.1; Mark 6.17; indirectly Mark 8.27; Matthew 16.13) do not name him among the evil members of the Herodian family, although he married Salome, the daughter of Herodias and Herod Antipas, who had caused the death of John the Baptist.[20] Nevertheless, it may be assumed that Jesus and his disciples felt safe in his territory.

They walked the road from Bethsaida to Caesarea at least once (Mark 8.22 with 8.27). The direct road, more or less following the course of the River Jordan, was just under fifty kilometres long – a two to three days' journey, depending on their speed and determination. On the occasion mentioned by Mark, it took them at least a day longer, for on their way they stopped to find out who people thought Jesus was (Mark 8.27). It could be called the first 'opinion poll' known from clas-sical sources. The fame of Jesus had spread from Galilee, where even someone like Herod Antipas had thought he was John the Baptist reborn (Matthew 14.1–2), into Gentile regions. And the Jews in the mainly pagan Gaulanitis were an interesting target group for such a survey. Isolated within a non-Jewish environment, their hopes and expectations were more acute than elsewhere in the Holy Land; the everyday reality of a pro-Roman government permeated by pro-Greek culture sharpened their awareness of their Jewish identity. One of Jesus' disciples, Simon the Zealot (Luke 6.15; Acts 1.13), seems to have had nationalistic leanings. Zealotism may not have been militarily active in those years, but Josephus traces its origins back to the uprising of AD 6, when a certain Judas from Gamla in the Gaulanitis (see Acts 5.37) started a revolt by claiming that it amounted to high treason against God, Israel's true ruler, to pay tribute to an occupying emperor.[21] The city of Gamla was just twenty kilometres from Bethsaida, and the descendants of this Judas continued to shape the movement's activities while Jesus was active within walking distance; later, during the early stages of the devastating uprising of AD 66–73, Gamla became their most important stronghold until its final defeat by the Romans in AD 67, when 9,000 defenders died.[22] Eleazar, the heroic leader of the zealots on Masada, which fell at the end of the revolt in AD 73/4, was himself a descendant of Judas.[23] We should not ignore Judas and his movement, particularly at the time of Jesus, since it influenced the messianic thinking of many Jews not only in the Gaulanitis, but also in eastern Galilee.

Their fervent hope for a victorious Messiah who would defeat the Roman occupiers was infectious. Simon Peter, Andrew and Philip, the disciples who, before moving to Capernaum, had spent their formative years in Bethsaida – which was, like Gamla, in the tetrarchy of Philip – would have been susceptible to this popular movement. And in spite of the messianic teaching he received from Jesus, Simon Peter reverted to his old way of thinking in the Garden of Gethsemane, when he drew his sword and cut off the high priest's servant's right ear: clearly, in his eyes, the signal for the messianic, angelic hosts to begin the final eschatological battle.[24] Then, as earlier in Galilee, where Peter had refused to accept Jesus' self-definition as the suffering Messiah, Jesus corrected the disciple's error (Luke 22.51). It did not require divine powers for Jesus to have known who Simon the Zealot was, and how the disciples from Bethsaida would have felt and thought. Did he call them, and above all the Zealot, into his closer circle specifically in order to enlighten and re-educate them, and to prepare them for a future ministry in the wake of the true Messiah, Christ Jesus? If so, the end result was a real achievement: Simon the Zealot, Simon Peter, Andrew and

Philip became founding members of the apostolic community in Jerusalem (Acts 1.12–14).

An opinion poll and its consequences

With all this in mind, the 'opinion poll' on Jesus' ministry, taken on the way from Bethsaida to Caesarea Philippi, was a serious matter. It confirmed that the people of the Gaulanitis thought the same as those in the Galilean territory of Herod Antipas: 'Some were saying, "John the baptizer has been raised from the dead; and for this reason these powers are at work in him." But others said, "It is Elijah." And others said, "It is a prophet, like one of the prophets of old." But when Herod [Antipas] heard of it, he said, "John, whom I beheaded, has been raised"' (Mark 6.14–16). This is remarkably close to the poll in the northern half of Philip's territory: '"Who do people say that I am?" And they answered him, "John the Baptist; and others, Elijah; and still others, one of the prophets"' (Mark 8.27–8). Matthew, in his account of the survey, names 'one of these prophets': Jeremiah (Matthew 16.14). All those who had seen Jesus at work or had heard about him appear to admit that he had unusual abilities, but are not ready to accept that these powers are his own. However, the extent to which they are prepared to recognize him is revolutionary enough in itself. The Baptist, Elijah and the prophets, Jeremiah above all, had one thing in common: they were preachers of repentance. They proclaimed the judgement of God on a society which lacked any awareness of its sinfulness, and any willingness to repent and 'turn around' (which is what the Greek word *metanoeō*, 'repent', literally means). And they not only preached; they opened up ways and perspectives. John the Baptist, a relative of Jesus (since their mothers were related: Luke 1.36), introduced the most radical step, a visible act of confession and commitment, in physical purification by baptism. John's baptism was no invitation to immerse oneself, as Elisha had ordered Naaman to do seven times in the Jordan. He himself performed the act, among witnesses. This was new and differed completely from the regular, repeated self-purification of the Essenes at Qumran.[25] Followers and admirers of the Baptist may have found it difficult to accept his death; seeing him as having been reborn in Jesus, as one of the heralds of the Messianic Age, was a sign of hope.[26] In any case, identifying him with John the Baptist was a form of acknowledgement; after all, Jesus himself had called him the greatest among the prophets and the greatest among men (Matthew 11.9–11).

As for the prophets, Jesus himself saw the line which linked the Baptist to prophecy fulfilled: 'See, I am sending my messenger to prepare the way before me' (Malachi 3.1). Jesus combined it with Exodus 23.20 and praised the Baptist: 'This is the one about whom it is written, "See, I am sending my messenger ahead of you, who will prepare your way before you"' (Matthew 11.10). In other words, he accepted that the Baptist had come to prepare the way for him, the Christ. And he went on to link the Baptist with the one man singled out by name in both 'surveys' – at the court of Herod Antipas and in the Gaulanitis – as one of the messianic precursors: Elijah. 'And if you are willing to accept it, he is Elijah who is to come. Let anyone with ears listen!' (Matthew 11.14–15, 17.10–13) Elijah's place was well established among Jews in those days. The prophet Malachi himself had laid the foundation for it: 'Lo, I will send you the prophet Elijah before the great and terrible day of the LORD comes. He will turn the hearts of parents to their children and the hearts of children to their parents, so that I will not come and strike the land with a curse' (Malachi 5.5–6). This is how the Old Testament ends in our Christian Bibles.[27] Elijah and John the Baptist share several characteristics, and John must have wanted this to be apparent – he clothed himself like Elijah (2 Kings 1.8), without pretending to be one and the same in the sense of a reincarnation: 'And they asked him, "What then? Are you Elijah?" He said, "I am not"' (John 1.21). In other words, as Jesus and the Baptist agreed, there was a visible line linking Elijah to the Baptist, justifying a spiritual and moral likeness, but neither Jesus nor the Baptist accepted the possibility of reincarnation, a notion which was popular among Jews at the time and remains a widespread idea among orthodox Jews today. And it was obvious to anyone who had seen John in action that he had said and done things which had not been credited to Elijah. In a prophetic tradition, he was a new and radical precursor of the Messiah.

So much is evident, then: if there were people who recognized the character and qualities of John the Baptist in Jesus, it was, primarily, a very Jewish appreciation, without so much as a hint of Hellenistic influence; and at the same time, it was a dramatic admission – the last days, the Messianic Age promised by God through his prophets, was deemed near. Was it a threat to religious peace – as Herod Antipas, the murderer of John the Baptist, must have thought, or was it the breakthrough, after so many decades of suppression by the Romans, as the Zealots among the Jews must have hoped? Jesus certainly understood that both these views were dangerous and avoided the vicinity of Herod's centres of power; thus he never stayed in Herod's new capital, Tiberias, and people from Tiberias had to take a boat to get to his preferred sites, which were close enough to the safer territory of Philip (John 6.23). It was a justified precaution; not much later, Jesus was warned by some Pharisees: 'Get away from here, for Herod wants to kill you' (Luke 13.31).

In the 'opinion poll' in the northern Gaulanitis other prophets were also alluded to, and, as we saw, Jeremiah was singled out by name. Why him? It was Jeremiah who had prophesied God's judgement and the destruction of the First Temple, who had been persecuted and who nonetheless spoke of hope in God's help when his prophecies had come true. Above all, the shorter of his two books, the Lamentations, speaks a very individual, unmistakable language. In the Hebrew Bible, this book is called 'Ekha', after its first word, meaning 'Woe'.[28] To this day, the 9th of Av, or 'Tisha be'Av', which tends to be in late July/early August in the Jewish calendar, is an important day for Jews worldwide, commemorating the destruction of the First Temple in 586 BC, and of the Second Temple in AD 70. And on that day, the book of Lamentations is read, from beginning to end, in synagogues everywhere. When Jesus appeared on the scene, the book was already six hundred years old. And it was this Jeremiah who came to the mind of devout Jews when they saw Jesus, who in turn knew the book and quoted from it.[29] Jesus' prophecy of impending disaster, his call to repentance and his compassion for the plight of his own people made him appear like a new Jeremiah in the eyes of many Jews. For many a wandering rabbi, the results of this survey would have been a remarkable success. However, unique as it was in the first century – no other Jew received comparable 'rankings' – it was a double-edged sword. Seen from the position of Jesus himself, they obviously underestimated him, and seen from the position of those Jews, he was profoundly misunderstood to be the last of the pre-messianic prophets who would herald the coming of the victorious Messiah, the violent conqueror of all oppressors from without and within.

While the results of the opinion poll were coming in, the group approached Caesarea. Mark is very precise in his account: they did not reach Caesarea itself, the inhabited city, but the outskirts, or, as he puts it, 'the villages of Caesarea Philippi' (8.27). The district of Caesarea (as Matthew calls it, 16.13) was a conglomeration of villages and farmsteads. Why is Mark's precision so important for a proper understanding of what happens next? Those of his (and Matthew's) readers who had heard about Caesarea or had been there themselves would have known one thing about it. On the outskirts of the city, before one reached the villages and the city itself, there stood the most important shrine to the Greek god Pan in the eastern Roman Empire. There also was a temple of Augustus and Roma, built by Herod the Great, but it was one of many similar temples in the Holy Land and in dozens of towns elsewhere. The shrine of Pan at Caesarea, however, was one of the most popular pilgrimage sites in those days. It had been called 'Paneas' before Philip the Tetrarch renamed it in honour of Augustus, the Caesar, and after a brief spell when it was called 'Neronias' during the latter years of Nero's reign, it regained its ancient name and has retained it into the twenty-first century: Arab Israelis frequent its spacious parks and impressive waterfall as one of their favourite weekend destinations, and they call it 'Banyas'. Coming from the direction of Bethsaida, Jesus and the disciples were precisely in this area when Jesus asked them about the outcome of the poll and continued with the all-decisive follow-up: 'Who do you say that I am?'

Some Jews lived in Caesarea itself, but they preferred to avoid the outskirts. The pagan accessories of the imperial cult and the Grecian pilgrimage site did not attract them. Josephus, ever the conciliatory voice between Roman and Jewish sensitivities, pointed out that it was near the sources of the Jordan, the archetypal Jewish river which ran through the promised land from north to south.[30] But even he could not lessen the overall effect of a place where pagans met to venerate the emperor and to worship the god Pan, whose cave had been here at least since the Hellenization of the Levant in the fourth century BC. Pan, after all, was not just any Graeco-Roman deity. His myth began in Arcadia, and the sources describe him as half man, half goat, looking after the herds, with a syrinx, the 'pan-pipes', in his hand. Eventually, he became the god of fertility, and he was credited with the invention of 'Pan-ic', panic, sowing sudden fear among the enemies of the Greeks. As early as Homer's 'Hymn to Pan', he was linked with the Greek word *pān*, which means 'all', and thus he became the universal 'All God' in popular worship. And it is this cult of the 'All God', widespread in New Testament times, which made the site of Paneas/Caesarea Philippi so challenging, and at the same time attractive, to Jesus. At one stroke, he could take the real presences of the imperial cult and of pagan myth into the scope of his divine vision, and he could do so at one of the sources of the Jordan, the river of Judaism.

The question 'But who do you say that I am?', when asked at this site, becomes a religious, philosophical and political question. Jesus and the disciples saw the temple of Augustus, they saw the caves and the shrine of Pan, and they saw the Jordan. The whole ensemble has been re-excavated in recent years, and we can see how Jesus used the visible structures to charge his words with multiple meaning. Simon Peter's confession, 'You are the Christ, the Son of the living God' (Matthew 16.16) is anything but a late invention of Christianity after Easter, as some scholars apparently still believe. It sums up what he and the others had seen and heard, and it incorporates the architecture of the site. '*You* are', he says and implies that the widespread appreciation of Jesus they had just observed in their survey was incomplete. The waiting was over. 'You *are*' – it was the moment to accept and confirm the voice from heaven which some had witnessed at the baptism of Jesus: 'This is my Son, the Beloved, with whom I am well pleased' (Matthew 3.17). Jesus was the Messiah, the true Anointed One of God, and he was God's Son. Whether or not Simon Peter was interested in the biological corollaries of such a statement cannot concern us here. What mattered to him, first and foremost, was the immediate, almost tangible link between the imperial cult on the one hand, and Jewish faith on the other. The temple of Augustus was the temple of a son of God, as we saw in Chapter 3. But Augustus, like his successors, was the man-made son of a dead and man-made divinity. And thus, Matthew makes sure, in his extended version of the event, that we get Simon Peter's point in its entirety: Jesus is 'the Son of the *living* God' (Matthew 16.16).

At one stroke, this statement throws down the gauntlet to the emperors and their official cult, and reaffirms the age-old faith in God's ordinances. The God of the Jews is a living God (Psalm 42.3, 84.3; Jeremiah 10.10; Daniel 6.27; etc.). If demons were afraid of this Son (remember the incident near Gadara, Matthew 8.29), if Roman emperors had to be challenged in their blasphemous arrogance, if Jesus could see himself in these terms even before the question at Caesarea Philippi (Matthew 11.25–7), why hesitate any longer? Simon Peter was not unprepared. According to John's Gospel, he had previously realized who Jesus was – 'the Holy One of God' (John 6.68–9). After a moment of mortal danger on the lake, all the disciples had expressed their awe and admiration: 'You are truly the Son of God!' (Matthew 14.33). Now, however, neither fear, nor relief, nor any other spontaneous reaction was called for. Jesus asks the decisive question, and Simon Peter responds with an unequivocal proclamation.

Jesus and the disciples probably spoke Aramaic on this occasion, rather than Greek. And yet, in his reply, Jesus demonstrates once more his familiarity with both of these everyday languages and their cultural backgrounds: 'Blessed are you, Simon Bar Jonah. For flesh and blood has not revealed this to you, but my Father in heaven. And I tell you, you are Peter, and on this rock I will build my church' (Matthew 16.17–18). The address is decidedly Jewish. Simon, Symeōn or Shimon, was the first name, and in Jewish nomenclature the name of the father, or the place of origin, was added to identify further the bearer of the name. 'Bar' means 'son' in Aramaic, and Jonah was a well-known male name, famous not least because of one of the Twelve Minor Prophets, the book of Jonah. John in his Gospel calls Simon's father 'Iōannēs', which is 'Yoannan' in Aramaic, or 'Johanan'/'John' in English (John 1.42, 21.15–17), but readers of the Greek Bible knew of course that Jonah and Johanan were in fact the same name, and that Jonah could be understood as the shorter form of Johanan: in 2 Kings 25.23, the Septuagint has 'Jonah' instead of 'Johanan'.[31] Thus the sources agree, and they also confirm that the father's name was Jewish. This is noteworthy for a simple reason: in Jewish society, it was the father's responsibility to name the children.[32] And Jonah/Johanan named his two sons Andrew and Simon. Andrew is an entirely Greek name, 'Andreas' in Greek, 'the manly one'. Simon is Jewish enough, at first glance, but it is also Greek: a non-Jewish friend of the philosopher Socrates, for example, was called Simon, and is mentioned in Aristophanes' comedy *The Clouds* as early as *c.* 423 BC.[33] He was a cobbler, and his shop has been identified by archaeologists near the Athenian agora.[34] The least one can say, therefore, is this: the father gave his two sons cross-cultural names. In Bethsaida, in Philip's Hellenistic tetrarchy, this was an understandable decision.

Rocks of ages

And what is more, Simon's byname also works in both languages and cultures. 'Peter' is 'Petros' in Greek, and Jesus appears to play with words: 'You are Peter', he says, 'and on this rock [Greek *petra*] I will build my church.' Obviously, he could not have given a female name, 'Petra', to a male apostle, so we read the Greek male form, 'Petros'. But if Jesus spoke in Aramaic, the word would have been *kêphâ(s)*, which means rock, solid stone, and is documented as a male Jewish name, 'Ahab Bar Kêphâ', in a papyrus found among pre-Christian Jewish documents on the island of Elephantine in Upper Egypt.[35] And a surprising discovery among the Dead Sea Scrolls proves the existence of the Greek form, Petros, even among Aramaic-speaking Jews some time before the dialogue at Caesarea Philippi took place. The leather fragment 4QM130, an Aramaic writing exercise in the form of several names like Aquila, Dallui, Eli, Gaddi, Hyrcanus, Jannai, Magnus, Malkiha, Mephisbosheth, Zakariel – in other words, Hebrew, Aramaic, Greek and even Latin names – includes Petros, in a precise Aramaic transcription of the Greek spelling.[36] It is safe to say that Jesus did not have to invent the name and its Greek form. Jews knew it and used it, even in a cross-cultural writing exercise.

In fact, it is quite probable that Simon must have been known as 'Simon Peter' before his messianic proclamation. There is the earlier scene, a couple of days after Jesus' baptism, reported by John:

> One of the two who heard John speak and followed him was Andrew, Simon Peter's brother. He first found his brother Simon and said to him, 'We have found the Messiah' (which is translated Anointed). He brought Simon to Jesus, who looked at him and said, 'You are to be called [or, You will be called] Cephas' (which is translated Peter). (John 1.40–2)

For the historian, there is no reason to assume that John and the other three Gospel authors wrote about the same naming incident and simply placed it in different contexts. On the contrary, John's sentence structure is unmistakable. Immediately after his baptism, Jesus promised

69

Peter that – one day – he would be called 'the rock'. Remarkably, Jesus said this just after meeting Peter for the first time. For John, this was good enough: writing at a time when everyone knew that Simon was indeed called Peter in the early Christian community, he did not feel the need to mention the Caesarea episode as well. Conversely, Mark, Matthew and Luke came to a different decision, omitted the earlier moment and focused on the decisive later event when Jesus confirmed Simon's calling. Taking the evidence of all four Gospels together, we realize that they are not in disagreement. All we might add, between the lines as it were, is a 'now truly' at Caesarea: 'And I tell you, now you are truly Peter'. In any case, 'Petros' remains a byname. Even after Caesarea, Jesus always calls him 'Simon', never 'Simon Peter' or just 'Peter'. It was left to Paul to use 'Kêphâs' as if it were a personal name, and it was the Gospel authors' decision, in their narrative passages, occasionally to call Simon merely 'Petros'. The byname became a title of honour which in turn became a personal name – this is just what happened to Jesus himself, whose title 'the Messiah', the 'Christos', evolved into a kind of byname, 'Jesus Christ', and finally, more often than not in the history of Christianity, has been used like a personal proper name.

The 'rock' of Peter was of course an old biblical concept. Abraham was called the rock by Isaiah (51.1–2), and even God could be called the rock, in 2 Samuel 22.3. In the Septuagint, *petra* is the appropriate translation. This multilingual cross-fertilization, working successfully and convincingly in at least two languages, sometimes in three (Aramaic, Greek and Hebrew), does not end here. The next controversial word again presupposes an acute awareness of meanings in more than one language. 'On this rock', Jesus goes on, 'I will build my church' (Matthew 16.18). There has been a controversy among Protestant and Roman Catholic scholars about the subject of this statement: was Jesus referring to Peter himself, or merely to his faith in Jesus as the Messiah and the Son of God? These days, the majority of Protestants seems willing to agree that Jesus did mean Peter.[37] But what about the 'church'? Many still assume that the historical Jesus could not possibly have spoken of a church. It must be an invention of the early community after Easter, put into the mouth of Jesus. Really? In Matthew's Greek text, we read *ekklēsía*. It recognizably reappears in the English word 'ecclesiastical', which carries the burden of hundreds of years of church history. But in the original Greek, it has a harmless beginning. The *ekklēsía* was an assembly of citizens, convened on a regular basis.[38] In the pre-Christian Greek Old Testament, it usually means an assembly, and in several cases, the community of Israel (Deuteronomy 4.10, 23.2; Psalm 22.23, 149.1; Joel 2.16; etc.).

In other words, the term was in common use among Greek-speaking Jews at least two centuries before Matthew recorded it. And given the likelihood that Jesus spoke Aramaic at Caesarea Philippi, he would have used *qâhâl*. It is the original biblical word for this community, and it was common enough even in contemporary Jewish thought to occur several times in the Dead Sea Scrolls.[39] Either way, no Jewish reader, and no Gentile reader for that matter, could have misunderstood Jesus. The term worked in both languages, and what is more, the concept behind it was both self-evident and a necessity: if Jesus was the Messiah, if Peter proclaimed him as such, how could anyone have assumed for a moment that this Messiah could spread his message without a messianic community? The mere thought would have been a contradiction in terms. It was left to the anti-historical interpreters of the Gospels to come up with the nonsensical idea of a post-Easter invention. Needless to say, we may ask if Jesus envisaged, let alone wanted, the church(es) as we have them today, but it would be irresponsible to impose a modern sense of dissatisfaction on mid-first-century realities.

Finally, and returning to the geography of Caesarea Philippi, we are surrounded by remarkable scenery. The rock of Peter, be it in Aramaic or in Greek, was a Jewish notion, but Jesus used it in front of the shrine of Pan, which was built into a vast, visually overpowering rockface. There was Pan, with his caves, and with the niches for auxiliary gods like Echo and other nymphs which can still be seen today. And there was Peter, the new rock on which the messianic community of Jesus was to be built. 'On *this* rock I will build,' Jesus said, and his words were a challenge to the Graeco-Roman world of gods and demigods. The system which had engendered a being like Pan and his rock at Caesarea was defeated. Jesus reciprocated Peter's proclamation. If Peter had announced the messianic victory over the spurious sons of God and their imperial cult, now Jesus announced that the rock of Peter meant the overcoming of pagan religion. 'And the gates of Hades will not prevail against it,' Jesus added (Matthew 16.18). The expression was taken from Isaiah 38.10, where the gates of Sheol signify the realm of death.[40]

Jewish listeners and readers understood immediately: the new community will not die out, the powers of death are no match for it. And at the same time, the deep, dark cave of the pagan shrine reminded the disciples, and any of the many readers of the Gospel who knew the site, of the intended double meaning. Pan, the 'All God', whose mythical history had always been connected with caves, was no threat. Pan was dead, he and the other cults were of no relevance. The emperor's temple was dead stone, a symbol which had no future. By going to Caesarea Philippi, Jesus turned the moment he had chosen, the messianic proclamation, into a religious and political statement. Graeco-Roman mythology and the imperial cult had permeated the world of Jews and non-Jews alike. Against this all-powerful reality, Jesus did not take the road of 'inner emigration', withdrawing into a non-political Judaism with a kind of internal message for Jews only. He challenged all strata of Gentile and Jewish societies, he resisted, and he provoked. The historical moment at Caesarea was to change the world. Fittingly, he ordered the disciples 'not to tell anyone that he was the Messiah' (Matthew 16.20). They knew who he was. The Romans and their vassals, Herod Antipas, Herod Agrippa, and hypocrites like Caiaphas would have to wait. The moment and place of the final confrontation was not to be decided by them.

5 Life after Death? Charon's Coin and Boxes for Bones in Jerusalem

> All religious language is symbolic in that it attempts to bridge the gap between the describable and the inexpressible, but that doesn't mean it's untrue. Quite the reverse.
>
> Susan Howatch, *Glamorous Powers*

> Then he said to me: 'Mortal, these bones are the whole house of Israel. They say, "Our bones are dried up, and our hope is lost; we are cut off completely." Therefore prophesy, and say to them, Thus says the Lord GOD: I am going to open your graves, and bring you up from your graves, O my people; and I will bring you back to the land of Israel.'
>
> Ezekiel 37.11–12

Telling others

A cosmopolitan north, the proverbial 'Galilee of the Gentiles' (Isaiah 8.23), thoroughly Romanized by Herod the Great and Herod Antipas, and the Hellenistic territories of Philip the Tetrarch: this, surprising though it may seem at first sight, does not pose a threat to the traditional idea of a provincial, Hebrew- and Aramaic-speaking Judaism. In a sense, what really mattered was Jerusalem and Judaea; the north was suspect to many Jews who lived south of Sychar (John 4.5). The real surprise, therefore, is the overwhelming evidence for a multilingual, multicultural Jerusalem at the time of Jesus. The Temple, of course, was the focal point for Jews the world over. But ironically, it was this unique position which internationalized Jerusalem. At the major festivals, Rosh ha-Shana (the Jewish New Year), Yom Kippur (Day of Atonement), Shukkot (Tabernacles), Passover, and Shavuot (Feast of Weeks, Pentecost), literally millions of pilgrims came from the Diaspora countries to visit the homeland, 'Eretz Israel', and to pray at the Temple.[1] Passover and Pentecost were the two most important occasions for pilgrims from abroad. The impressive Shavuot/Pentecost list of regions in

Acts 2.8–11 is entirely trustworthy. Other popular festivals like Hanukkah and Purim also attracted visitors. Hanukkah, in December, was not ordained by Holy Scripture, but it commemorated the re-consecration of the Temple under the Maccabeans in 164 BC (cf. the apocryphal books of 1 Maccabees 4.51–9 and 2 Maccabees 10.1–8, preserved in the Septuagint). And Purim, a joyous occasion celebrated on the 15th of Adar (usually in March), though not a biblically ordained festival, was recommended in two books which were widely read among Greek-speaking Jews (2 Maccabees 15.37, in memory of Queen Esther courageously rescuing the Jews in Persia as celebrated in Esther 9.19–32). Even after the destruction of Jerusalem and the Temple, the Talmud tells all male Jews to get drunk at Purim, until they can no longer distinguish between 'Arur Haman' (cursed be Haman) and 'Barukh Mordekhai' (blessed be Mordecai).[2]

The common language of all these pilgrims was Greek. We also know that Greek-speaking visitors asked for Jesus in Jerusalem, in the days before the Passover of AD 30 (John 12.20–1). All such visitors would have been able to stay at the guest houses of one of the entirely Greek-speaking synagogues. Several such synagogues of Hellenistic Jews are documented. Most famous among the finds is the Greek inscription of 'Theodotos, [son] of Vettenos' which is on display at the John Rockefeller Museum in Jerusalem.[3] Theodotos 'constructed the synagogue for the reading of the law and the teaching of the commandments and the guest room and the chambers and the installation of water for a hostelry for those needing them from abroad'. Apart from the archaeological evidence, there are further references to synagogues in Jerusalem before AD 70 (Acts 24.12), and to at least one further Greek-speaking or 'Hellenistic' one, frequented by the 'freedmen and the Cyrenians, those from Cilicia and Asia' (Acts 6.9). Apparently, they were Jews who had returned from the Diaspora countries, perhaps a generation or two before we encounter them in Acts, always ready to welcome pilgrims from their former homelands. The Cyrenians are particularly interesting. One of them, Simon from Cyrene, carried the cross for Jesus, and his two sons, Alexander and Rufus, later became members of the Jewish-Christian community (Mark 15.21).[4] In other words, even the cross of Jesus – or, to be precise, the horizontal bar of the cross – was carried by a Greek-speaking Jew. Since their synagogue is mentioned in the passage about Stephen and the Hellenists, and since some of its members object to Stephen's teaching without as much as a hint at his own (former) adherence to their group, we may assume that Stephen and the other Greek-speaking 'deacons' had originally belonged to yet another Hellenistic synagogue in Jerusalem. This should not surprise us. Jerusalem, in those days, was a metropolis where local Jews, those who had immigrated from abroad, seasonal tourists and pro-Jewish 'God-fearers' mixed, sharing in the teaching of the Bible, but reading the Greek translation, the Septuagint, and using Greek as their everyday language of worship and communication.

One of the many historical inaccuracies in Mel Gibson's much-vaunted movie *The Passion of the Christ* (2004) is the lack of Greek. Gibson used Latin and Aramaic as the languages spoken in the film, but in Jerusalem no one, not even the Romans, spoke Latin in public, which was used solely for administrative business, official documents and declarations. They all spoke Greek. The Jewish authorities were at pains to avoid desecrations of the inner Temple precincts by the presence of non-Jewish, uncircumcised visitors – a very real danger, given the sizeable number of the philo-semites called 'God-fearers' by Luke and Josephus, who attended the synagogues, read the Greek Bible, followed Jewish customs, but stopped short of converting and undergoing circumcision.[5] At least two barrier-stones were built for them at the Temple, both rediscovered by archaeologists. They were inscribed in one language only: Greek. And the message was unambiguous: 'No foreigner is to enter within the balustrade and enclosure around the Temple area. Whoever is caught will have himself to blame for his death which will follow.'[6] Paul was nearly killed because pious Jews suspected that he had taken an uncircumcised non-Jew, Trophimus, with him into the Temple (Acts 21.27–31). And obviously, his accusers assumed that he should have been able to understand the Greek interdiction.

Perhaps the most striking example for the use of languages in Jerusalem during this period is the inscription on the cross of Jesus, the so-called *titulus*. The Roman prefect Pontius Pilate had ordered a headboard to be attached to the cross, in compliance with Roman legal custom, where it was common to publish the 'reason for the punishment', the *causa poenae*, in such a way.[7] The description in John's Gospel – an eyewitness account (John 19.35) – gives the most complete version of the headboard: 'Jesus the Nazorean the King of the Jews' –

and 'it was written in Hebrew, Greek, and Latin' (John 19.19–20).[8] Some scholars have suggested that 'Hebrew' should be understood as 'Aramaic', but Hebrew makes sense, as the religious language of the crucified and his accusers who wanted him to be found guilty of a religious offence. Greek, the middle of the three languages on the *titulus*, was central in more senses than one. It was, as we have seen, the lingua franca of those several thousands of visitors to Jerusalem, many of whom could not avoid going past the site of the crucifixion, as it was close to the (western) main gate of the city (John 19.17–20; Hebrews 13.12). Latin followed last. Neither the local Jews nor the pilgrims needed it to understand the headboard, but the crucifixion was, after all, an official Roman act, and the Latin line was therefore obligatory at the end, almost like the prefect's signature.

The plot thickens when we look at the case of final rites and funeral inscriptions. Unlike in ancient Rome or modern Britain, where elaborate texts excite the collectors of curiosa as much as students of sociology, inscribed tombs and tombstones for Jews in and around Jerusalem were very rare at the time of Jesus. Even where ancient tombs may pre-date Jesus, inscriptions were mostly added later. A fascinating case study was made public in the autumn of 2003. The Israeli archaeologist and anthropologist Joseph E. Zias, a member of the Science and Antiquity Group at the Hebrew University of Jerusalem, discovered an inscription which people had failed to spot for some 1,600 years. It identified the so-called Tomb of Absalom in the Kidron Valley as the tomb of Zechariah, the father of John the Baptist.

Zechariah, called Zacharias in the Authorized Version, is one of those Christian saints who never had a chance to become a Christian, among them his son John the Baptist (feast days 24 June, Nativity, and 29 August, Beheading). Zechariah himself, and his wife Elizabeth, share a feast day (5 November). It cannot be denied that these three had pivotal roles to play when the stage was set for Jesus and his followers. John's position is obvious enough; even Flavius Josephus mentions him at length.[9] His parents are singled out by Luke (Luke 1.5–79). Both are called 'righteous before God'; they were *zaddikim*, the highest accolade anyone could bestow on devout, practising Jews. Obviously, Luke did not invent this epithet; he must have encountered it when he interviewed the eyewitnesses and contemporaries (cf. Luke 1.2–3). And it is not only the husband, i.e. the man, who is called a *zaddik*. Luke extends the traditionally male term also to the woman. Elizabeth, or rather, in Hebrew, 'Elisheba', which means 'My God is Perfection' (cf. Exodus 6.23), was a descendant of Aaron (Luke 1.5). This means, by definition, that John the Baptist himself was a descendant of the Aaronic priestly line. Zechariah, in Hebrew 'Zekarya' or 'Zekaryahu', 'God (YHWH) remembers', is introduced as a priest who belonged to 'the priestly order of Abijah' (Luke 1.5). Most readers do not stop to ponder what this means. The priestly order of Abijah was the eighth 'division' of the twenty-four (1 Chronicles 24.7–18) which were reinstituted after the Babylonian Exile (Nehemiah 12.1–7). Following a rota system, each division had to serve at the Temple for one week every six months. Among the members of each division, there was another rota, decided by the casting of lots, for the priests who had to burn the incense offering on the altar in the inner Temple twice a day (cf. Exodus 30.1–10). Luke tells us that on a given day, it was Zechariah's turn, when an angel of the Lord appeared to him and told him that his wife, barren and elderly, would bear him a son (Luke 1.11–13). As a 'Righteous one' and as a priest at the Temple, Zechariah was terrified by holy fear when he saw the angel (1.12), but knowledgeable enough to ask for a sign to confirm that the angel was a true and truthful messenger of the Lord (1.18). The sign is granted: he becomes mute. Leaving the sanctuary, he tries to explain to the others, by 'motioning to them', what had happened inside. The sight of the trusted man, awe-struck and unable to speak, motioning helplessly, convinced them that he had seen a vision in the sanctuary (1.22).

This muteness is followed later by another instructive incident. On the eighth day after the birth of their son, they are preparing to name him. In those days, it was a tradition to choose the father's or grandfather's name, and the relatives were apparently expecting 'Zechariah'. Elizabeth, still able to speak of course, tells them that he is to be called John, a new name in the family. They wish to hear what name Zechariah intends to give him. And he does what he must have done when he explained the angel's message to her months before: he asks for a writing tablet and writes 'His name is John' (1.63). Again, as in the technical and liturgical details about Zechariah's role and duties, Luke is precise and correct. The Greek word he uses for 'writing tablet' is *pinakidion*, a small tablet of wood, with a waxed surface, for brief notes which could be erased with the broad end of the stylus. It is in fact the only verse in the whole New Testament where this technical term is used. The people around Zechariah are amazed, not because he knows how to handle a writing tablet and is able to write, but because he confirms the name of John, and immediately, 'his mouth was opened and he began to speak'. His writing skills are not amazing at all – as we saw in the previous chapter, all male Jews, let alone members of one of the twenty-four chosen 'families' – were taught reading, writing, and memorizing techniques at the synagogal schools, and, much like today, some pupils were better than others. But writing as such, in more than one language (Hebrew, Aramaic and Greek must be assumed for Jews in public positions at that time), was an obligatory skill.

Zechariah pronounces a prophecy which is still used in churches at Morning Prayer as a hymn of praise, the Benedictus (Luke 1.68–79). It is a very Jewish text, full of quotes from and allusions to Old Testament writings, but, decisively, it uses these allusions in a new, truly prophetic context. And thus, even though the New Testament does not mention him anywhere after this prophecy, and we never find him among the early lists of earnest followers of Christ Jesus, he became a true saint of the Church. But what happened to him later? The mid- to late second-century *Proto-Gospel of James* offers an explanation: allegedly, Zechariah was killed in the forecourt of the Temple, by command of Herod 'the Great', at some stage between 7 and 4 BC.[10]

Legend or not, something more substantial was to turn up in the summer of 2002: authentic evidence for the early veneration of his tomb in Jerusalem. Tourists who have visited the Kidron Valley know about Zechariah's Tomb – but the pyramid-roofed tomb so named must be dated to the second century BC, and an inscription above the two columns identifies it as belonging to another priestly family, that of the Bene (Sons of) Hezir (cf. 1 Chronicles 24.15). However, fifty metres further north, there is the so-called Tomb of Absalom. It has had all sorts of odd names, among them the Arabic 'Tantour Firaoum', which means 'the Pharaohs' hat'. A medieval pilgrim, Benjamin of Tudela, was the first to describe it as Absalom's tomb, thinking of 2 Samuel 18.18 ('Now Absalom in his lifetime had taken and set up for himself a pillar that is in the King's Valley . . . It is called Absalom's Monument to this day.'). But the date is wrong: this tomb was built towards the end of the first century BC at the earliest. One day Joseph E. Zias suddenly discovered an inscription above the entrance. No one had noticed it before, as it can only be seen in the summer, in the light of the setting sun. Somewhat ironically, he explained that other scholars had failed to notice it because 'they knock off work at 3 pm'. High up on a ladder, Zias took a copy of the inscription, using latex (similar to the way dentists use it to take models of teeth). With the help of experts in ancient inscriptions, he identified the complete Greek text: 'This is the tomb of Zechariah the Martyr, the pious priest, father of John'. There can be no doubt – this is the Zechariah of Luke's Gospel. After further research into the archaeological and historical context, Zias was ready to publish his results in the autumn of 2002, but wisely decided to wait for the media turmoil about the forged ossuary of 'James, son of Joseph, brother of Jesus' to die down. Finally, he went public.[11]

A Christian author of the early sixth century, Archdeacon Theodosius, mentions a tomb near the Mount of Olives, where 'St James [the Lord's brother], St Zechariah and St Symeon' are buried; according to Theodosius, James himself had built this tomb, (re)buried the other two in it and left orders for his own remains to be buried there eventually.[12] The inscription rediscovered and identified by Zias is earlier than the travel report of Theodosius, from the mid- to late fourth century, and it only mentions Zechariah. Theodosius may have been over-enthusiastic in his account of prevailing local traditions, or further inscriptions mentioning the other two may have been destroyed, but in any case, the inscription of Zechariah is authentic, undoubtedly of the early Byzantine period, in the Greek style which was in use at the time. And it does tell us one thing: the early Church, when it began to look for biblical sites in the late fourth and early fifth centuries, found this to be the only site for which there existed a trustworthy tradition about the Baptist's father. Zias has been continuing his research at the tomb and has identified six lines with a large part of Luke 2.25 in a late fourth-century Greek style, apparently carved by laymen who followed the Greek text preserved in the mid-fourth-century Codex Sinaiticus: 'Now there was a man in Jerusalem whose name was Simeon; this man was righteous and devout, looking forward to the consolation of Israel, and the Holy Spirit rested on him.'[13] Thus, it looks as though the old tradition of a tomb shared by Zechariah with Sim(e)on, the author of the Nunc Dimittis (Luke 2.28–33), may be credible. Only a reference to James, the Lord's brother, has not been discovered so far. In any case, it is the first inscription with a New

Testament verse which has been found carved into a tomb anywhere in the Holy Land.[14]

To be sure, this does not mean that anyone can be certain that it really was the tomb of Zechariah and Simeon. All it does give us, if we remain cautious, is the fact that an early – indeed the earliest – local tradition identified this tomb, which became known as the Tomb of Absalom only seven centuries later, as that of Luke's Zechariah. And since the inscription is no later forgery, we have, at long last, a new discovery which will not be relegated to the scrap heap of forgeries and pseudo-biblical evidence for a gullible mass readership. And what may be even more important is that this inscription will help us to reconsider the importance of Zechariah of the priestly order of Abijah, the father of the Baptist and the author of the Benedictus.

Fascinating as this ongoing detective story is, we can also look for evidence even closer to the days of Jesus. And it does exist – not on tombs or tombstones, but on bone caskets, called 'ossuaries' in technical language (from Latin *os*, bone). Especially in and around Jerusalem at the time of the Second Temple, Jews reburied the bones of deceased men and women once the flesh had rotted away. They placed them in ossuaries to wait for the physical resurrection in the last days, at the end of time, according to the prophecies in Isaiah 26.19 and Ezekiel 37.11–12, quoted above as an epigraph to this chapter. And they really believed that this was more than a couple of prophecies of old. The Sadducees may have refused to accept the reality of a bodily resurrection (Mark 12.18; Acts 23.8, etc.),[15] but all the other Jews, the Pharisees not excluded, believed in it. Apart from the prophecies in Isaiah and Ezekiel, the Jewish hero Judas Maccabeus had buried the bodies of the fallen in 168 BC, 'taking account of the resurrection' (2 Maccabees 12.39–45), and even the orthodox Essenes accepted the physical reality of the risen body: 'The Lord will do glorious things which have not been done before, just as he said. Then he shall heal the pierced, and he shall revive the dead'.[16]

Getting ready for the resurrection

'My son, when I die, dump me first in a ditch. In the course of time [when the flesh has rotted away], collect my bones and bury them in an ossuary.' These are the words of a first-century rabbi, Elezar Bar

Zadok.[17] It was taught in the Talmud that the first burial in a tomb, which was usually hewn into a rock, with the body placed on benches or ledges, or in long and narrow niches, the so-called *kokim*, was only provisional: 'When the flesh was decomposed completely, the bones were gathered and buried in their proper place [i.e. the bone casket].'[18] It seems that the Talmud, which was composed and 'published' in the sixth century AD, remembered this custom, which was typical of the first centuries BC and AD. No one was excluded, not even Jews who had been executed. In 1968, archaeologists discovered an ossuary in northern Jerusalem, at Giv'at ha-Mivtar (called 'Ammunition Hill' in English); it contained the bones of a crucified Jew, Yehokhanan (John) ben Hazkul. The name was incised into the ossuary, and following the analysis of the bones, they were found to have belonged to a young man, about 25 years old, who had been crucified in *c.* AD 30. The nail driven through his right ankle-bone was a typical Roman *clavus trabalis*, 12 centimetres long, squared, with four sides of 0.9 centimetres each, and was still in place. It had fish-hooked and could not be extracted prior to his burial.[19] Jesus, provisionally buried in the new family tomb of Joseph of Arimathea, would have been given an ossuary burial, too, needless to say – but, as we know, something (and someone) intervened on the third day.

The flesh symbolized the sinfulness of the old body. Only the pure and dry bones were fit to expect the resurrection. And since this was the final burial, many ossuaries were beautifully decorated with rosettes, lines, circles, etc., carefully avoiding any depiction of real objects, in compliance with the Second Commandment. Many hundreds have been found with the names of the dead person on the lid, and/or on one of the sides. The incising or painting of the name was the final act, when the casket was in place, and was usually left to a member of the family; only a very few inscriptions were carried out by skilled scribes in professionally executed lettering. One would of course expect most if not all of these inscriptions to be in Aramaic, commonly accepted to have been the native tongue of Jerusalemites, or in liturgical Hebrew, but there are quite a few exceptions. And this is where we return to a family briefly mentioned above: Simon of Cyrene, the man who carried the horizontal beam of the cross of Jesus, and his sons Alexander and Rufus.

South of the City of David, today's Silwan village, there is the 'Mount of Offence', which is usually identified with the Mount of

Corruption in 2 Kings 23.13. In 1941, two leading archaeologists, Nahman Avigad and Eleazar Sukenik (the father of Yigael Yadin and one of the driving forces behind the recovery and acquisition of the Dead Sea Scrolls in the years after the accidental discovery of the first cave, by Bedouin arms smugglers, in 1947), discovered a tomb chamber on this hill, hewn into the rock, with bones and eleven ossuaries on shelves. A lamp and other pottery which belonged to the late Herodian period helped to date the chamber, even before the bones were analysed, to the first century AD. No one paid much attention to this discovery at the time: these were the difficult last years of the British Mandate, and scholars kept things very much to themselves. Nonetheless, the ossuaries were taken to the Palestine Archaeological Museum opposite Herod's Gate in East Jerusalem (today's John Rockefeller Museum), and one made its way to the Hebrew University on Mount Scopus. None of the eleven ossuaries was decorated, but nine had inscriptions. Avigad and Sukenik immediately noticed a striking ratio: only one was in Hebrew, one was in Hebrew and Greek, and the other seven only in Greek.[20] Was this the family tomb of a Greek-speaking Jewish family who only slowly began to see the point of adding or preferring Hebrew to their main language? A first clue was found on the Greek ossuary belonging to a 'Sarah [daughter] of Simon of Ptolemais'. Three cities of that name were known in the first century: one in south-eastern Syrophoenicia, better known today as Akko(n); another in Egypt; and the third in the Cyrenaica, a district of what is now eastern Libya. All three regions were Greek-speaking with minority Jewish populations. So which was it? The answer, and the real surprise, came when another of the ossuaries, the one at the Hebrew University, was analysed.

On the front, there was 'Alexander', written in green chalk, and in Greek only; on the back, 'Alexander' was incised, and again only in Greek. Both times, another name was added in the nominative, the same name as the one discovered on the ossuary of Sarah: 'Simon'. Apparently, the inexperienced scribe had needed several attempts to get the inscription right. He had not intended to say that both Alexander and Simon were in the ossuary, as the nominative cases on the front might have suggested. So he tried again on the back, but once more, he began with a mistake, writing 'Simon Ale' – and broke off. With Simon's name first, readers would have thought that Simon was Alexander's son.

He began a second line, with 'Alexander', and added a third line, 'of Simon'. Exceptionally, there was writing on the lid as well. First, there was 'Alexander', incised in large Greek letters, in the genitive, and not preceded or followed by another name. Thus inscribed, the lid marked this as being the ossuary 'of Alexander'. Underneath, in much smaller letters, the name was repeated in Hebrew, followed by the Hebrew transcription of the place name 'Cyrene'.[21] Alexander, the son of Simon, came from the capital of the Cyrenaica, and Sarah, in the other ossuary, was apparently a close relative, perhaps even a sister, from the city of Ptolemais in the same region.[22]

Surprisingly, this ossuary remained more or less unnoticed at the Hebrew University of Jerusalem until the present writer, as director of the scientific committee ('comitato scientifico') of an archaeological exhibition in Italy, applied for the loan of the casket. It was restored and in 1996 was presented for public viewing for the first time since its discovery in 1941. By the time of the exhibition, even the scholars at the Israel Antiquities Authority were convinced that the person buried there was none other than Alexander, son of Simon of Cyrene, mentioned in Mark 15.21.[23] Although Simon was a common name among Jews from the Diaspora and in the Holy Land, Alexander was much less frequent, and as for the combination of a father called Simon with a son called Alexander, with the indication of Cyrene as their place of origin, there is no other example.[24]

In other words, we have an archaeological object which confirms a passage in the New Testament, proves the bilingual culture of this family, and documents the continued use of ossuaries in the earliest Jewish-Christian community of Jerusalem, of which Alexander and his brother Rufus had become members. The ossuaries of Simon and Rufus have not been found in the tomb. The father could have died elsewhere, perhaps back home in Cyrene. Of Rufus, however, there may be a trace in Paul's letter to the Romans. 'Greet Rufus, chosen in the Lord, and greet his mother – a mother to me also,' we read in Romans 16.13. Rufus was not an uncommon name in Rome, so the link is tenuous, but the eminent scholar F. F. Bruce saw good reasons to accept the circumstantial evidence.[25] Nothing depends on this identification, however. The ossuary in itself is important enough for what it tells us, irrespective of what the family tomb where it was found may leave unanswered.

Beware the forger

The ossuary of Alexander was found by archaeologists *in situ*, which means at the actual site where it had always been until its rediscovery. In the light of a long and unpleasant history of forgeries designed to 'prove' biblical claims, this is an important fact. The classical historian is quite happy with textual documents having no archaeological under-pinning whatsoever – after all, the text is the primary source, and an archaeological object can, at best, contribute to a fuller understanding of the text. This is one of the reasons why philologists and historians of antiquity tend to smile at the attitude of many New Testament scholars who think that their 'hermeneutic of suspicion' toward the texts of the New Testament is a sign of enlightened scholarship. Quite the reverse. They, like all of us, will have to appreciate afresh that the credibility of these twenty-seven writings does not depend on outside corroboration, be it by non-Christian authors or by archaeological discoveries.[26] The ossuary of Alexander confirmed a reference in Mark's Gospel, and it widened the horizon, but the credibility of Mark's reference did not depend on its discovery. For the historian, there was no palpable reason to doubt the information provided in Mark 15.21 anyway. The topsy-turvy world of Gospel criticism became apparent in the autumn of 2003, when an ossuary of 'James, son of Joseph, brother of Jesus' was sensationalized by some media, worldwide, as being the first solid proof that Jesus ever existed. After all, these people thought, this was an ossuary, hence a real object, which could be trusted – unlike Matthew, Mark, Luke and John, or other classical authors, for that matter, like Josephus and Tacitus, who also mentioned Jesus as an historical person.[27]

The fallacy in an approach which relies on the tangible evidence of the ossuary is evident: without Matthew's Gospel (13.55) and Paul's let-ter to the Galatians (1.19) we would not even know that the combination James–Joseph–Jesus could refer to the leader of the Jerusalem commu-nity, his father Joseph and the Messiah Jesus. Matthew tells us what the people had said: Jesus was the 'son of the building worker', his mother was called Maria, and he had four brothers, James, Joseph, Simon and Judas, and several unnamed sisters. And Paul calls James 'the brother of the Lord'.[28] Otherwise, James, Joseph and John were among the twelve most popular Jewish male names, and in first-century Jerusalem alone, up to twenty families may have had a father and two sons with these names.[29] Imagine for a moment, if archaeologists were to find a tombstone in rural Berkshire, in two thousand years' time, with the inscription 'Charles, son of Philip, brother of Andrew', and nothing else. Would anyone seriously assume that these three were, beyond doubt, the Prince of Wales, the Duke of Edinburgh and the Duke of York in the early twenty-first century? Certainly not, since the determining indications of status and titles would be missing. And this is precisely what makes the ossuary from Jerusalem so useless for the historian. James who? Joseph who? Jesus who? The historical James was murdered in AD 62.[30] After the departure of Peter in AD 41/2 (Acts 12.17), James had apparently been the sole leader of the church in Jerusalem for twenty years. Everyone knew who he was, not least his enemies in the Sanhedrin who killed him. If then there were people who buried a certain James in an ossuary and, following tradition, added the name of the father, why should they have mentioned a brother's name as well? The only reason would have been to single out this particular James from among the many other Jameses with fathers called Joseph. But for us to assume, let alone know, that this Jesus was Jesus of Nazareth, among so many other bearers of that name in families with a James and a Joseph, something else is required: a title or definition of status. Remember, even Pontius Pilate did not just have 'Jesus' written on the headboard of the cross. Pilgrims and other passers-by were supposed to realize that the Jesus he was executing was Jesus of Nazareth.

What is more, we know from early Christian practice in the letters of the New Testament, written before the death of James as far as we can see today, that the first communities did not call the Risen and Ascended One just 'Jesus'. Apart from the epithet 'Lord', the prevailing style was 'Jesus the Christ' or 'the Christ Jesus', or simply 'the Christ'. Since 'Christ' is 'Messiah' in Hebrew/Aramaic, this is what we would have to expect on an authentic ossuary of the Lord's brother incised with an Aramaic inscription in late AD 62 or early AD 63: 'Brother of Jesus *ha Mashiakh* [the Messiah]. As this is missing, contrary to early Jewish-Christian custom, the ossuary is far too ambivalent to be of any historical use. Or, to put it differently, our primary sources, the Gospel of Matthew and Paul's letter to the Galatians, tell us more about these three people than this ossuary. Compare it to the case of the bilingual ossuary of Alexander, the son of Simon, from Cyrene: here, the archaeological find corroborates the Gospel account to the letter, and therefore can be used as a helpful piece of additional evidence.

Circumspect historians had immediately expressed reservations when the 'James' ossuary was made public in October 2002, and when another supposedly sensational find turned up a couple of months later, the so-called 'Joash' stele with a reference to the First Temple and its restoration. They warned that the numerous inconsistencies argued against authenticity, and specialists in Hebrew and Aramaic inscriptions pointed out that the 'Joash' text could not possibly be authentic, in view of the evident errors in the text. The empty ossuary had not been found *in situ*, but in the house of Oded Golan, an antique dealer; the stele had allegedly come from rubble removed by the Palestinian Wakhf during their illegal destruction of subterranean areas on Temple Mount. So who was fooled? It turned out to be those who trusted the *Biblical Archaeology Review* – a magazine which promoted the authenticity of the 'James' ossuary, relying heavily on the mistakes of an otherwise circumspect, well-known French epigrapher, André Lemaire – and those who bought the best-selling book by Hershel Shanks and Ben Witherington III.[31] As for the 'Joash' stele, those who mistakenly thought that the laughable claims of Palestinian propagandists and 'minimalist' archaeologists that there never was a (First) Temple on Temple Mount could be refuted by an inscription were equally misled.

The real problem, again, is one of methodology. As we saw above, public opinion has been undermined by an ideological, unscholarly majority trend in biblical research. People have been told that the Bible cannot and must not be trusted unless there is indisputable external evidence. For – or so ideology has it – if it is solely the Bible which tells us about a certain event with certain people occurring at a given place and time, it must be either theology or propaganda or both, but it is not history. If Josephus, the Jewish-Roman historian, appears to ignore or contradict a New Testament account, it is 'of course' Josephus who must be trusted, not the New Testament.[32] If Israelite accounts are not supported by Pharaonic accounts, they are, 'by definition', untrustworthy. If a predetermined chronology does not support the Bible (as in the recent dispute about the excavations at Megiddo), it is 'of course' the Old Testament which is wrong, not the predetermined chronology. And so forth, *ad nauseam*: small wonder that classical historians are beginning to dismiss the vested interests behind this amateurish attitude of many biblical scholars. After all, is there any other discipline in the study of antiquity where scholars begin, ideologically, by dismissing the intrinsic trustworthiness of their own sources? Of course there is none. And if, at this stage, some of those who have applied such hyper-critical approaches should object that their methodology is being caricatured, they should certainly be given the opportunity to present solid arguments in their defence. But the truth is that the public at large has been misled to believe that the historical accounts of the Bible (and, needless to say, not all the books of the Bible even claim to be histori-cal accounts!) cannot be trusted unless archaeology, or other forms of non-biblical evidence, support them. Just for the sake of argument, what about experimenting with an exercise in turning the tables? Cuneiform tablets and hieroglyphic accounts contain the opinions, beliefs and 'propaganda' of their authors and the masters behind them: Pharaonic, Hittite, etc. Is there any criterion which makes them more trustworthy than the opinions, beliefs and 'propaganda' of the biblical accounts? Definitely not. Thus, just for the fun of it, we could demand that any information about Pharaohs must not be trusted as historically reliable unless it is supported by biblical evidence.

Suggest this to an expert in ancient Egyptian history, and he or she will laugh. So too should all expert classical historians, who rely on those biblical accounts which explicitly claim to contain historical information, laugh at scholars who dismiss the Bible because it is the Bible. In terms of classical history, the biblical accounts are, by defini-tion, on a par with non-biblical accounts. They all have a story to tell, a message to proclaim. The Jewish claim that the Torah is God's Law, and the Judaeo-Christian claim that the Bible is God's word for all mankind, does not make these books any less credible than inscriptions about Pharaohs, the Gilgamesh epic, or whatever. This much should be obvi-ous to any enlightened observer of current debates.

Thus, back to those discoveries. Biblical evidence in favour of a First Temple and a King Joash with his repair work is solid enough. There is not a shred of textual evidence which might persuade a classical his-torian worth his or her salt to think otherwise. The stele, which has since turned out to be a forgery, would not have added to what we already know; it merely (mis)quoted a biblical account. And as for the ossuary of 'James, son of Joseph, brother of Jesus', we have already seen that, even if it had been authentic, it would have been of no particular use. In

87

other words, archaeological discoveries cannot 'prove' the Bible. In the best cases, they add visible evidence to the literary evidence of the texts. Assume for a moment that it was the other way round: no Matthew, no Galatians, but an (authentic) ossuary. We would not know what to make of it, and it would be relegated to the cellars of the Israel Antiquities Authority without further ado. As it happens, and in spite of the continuous efforts published in the *Biblical Archaeology Review* in support of its authenticity, the official analysis of the experts – two independent teams of eight scholars each, epigraphers, archaeologists, geologists and other specialists – which was carried out on behalf of the Israel Antiquities Authority confirmed the early suspicions of textual critics and historians: the bone casket as such is first century, but the inscription was added later, in two stages, perhaps as recently as the late twentieth century.[33] The forger was identified, his workshop was found on the roof of his house, the fact that he had forged both the 'James' ossuary and the 'Joash' stele was established, and when the police returned the valueless ossuary to him, he put it in his loo, as journalists from the Israeli newspaper *Haaretz* found, to their amusement, when they visited him.[34]

Archaeology does play a role in our understanding of Jesus and his cosmopolitan world. But it is important to get it right. And we have to acquire a new humility: New Testament research is subservient to the text. The text, those twenty-seven writings, is our primary source. Obviously, the same yardstick must be applied to the Old Testament. It is the text which defines our methods. Those who think that their methods determine the text and how to deal with it have decided to place themselves outside the community of classical scholarship. And archaeological information is merely one element of circumstantial evidence among so many others.

Playing safe

The real, historical James was a pious Jew, and he continued to worship at the Temple. His alleged ossuary, now shown to be a forgery, was faked by a man who was clearly too clever by half. James, or so he had heard, had been a Jew in the Mosaic tradition, who had opposed Paul's international Gentile mission and his targeting of the uncircumcised. The forger may even have heard of the stories which had circulated in early Christianity about James' devout Jewish prayer life which he maintained even as leader of the Jerusalem church:

> Alone he entered into the sanctuary [of the Temple], and was found on his knees asking forgiveness on behalf of his people, so that his knees became hard like a camel's, for he was continually bending his knee in worship to God, and asking forgiveness for the people. In fact, on account of his exceeding great justice he was called 'the Just' and 'Ōblías', which in Greek is 'bulwark of the people' and 'righteousness', as the prophets declare concerning him.[35]

So by imitating a first-century Aramaic writing style only and unaware of the bilingual evidence of the Alexander ossuary, the forger made the circle of James a monolingual group. On its own, the single language on the ossuary would not count as conclusive evidence of a forgery; in fact, it cannot be excluded that the circle of the real James might have incised his ossuary with only one language, be it Hebrew or Aramaic. But it is unlikely. For the point is this: forging a monolingual ossuary simply reiterates the erroneous image of a provincial, ultra-orthodox Jewish Christian community around James in Jerusalem which refused to look at broader developments, other languages, cultures and missionary target groups beyond the scope of their own messianic Judaism. As so often, the opposite picture is much more likely.

As the (half-)brother of Jesus, James had enjoyed the same upbringing in the same cosmopolitan environment as Jesus himself. He knew Hebrew, Aramaic, Greek; he could read and write; and while remaining an observant Jew, he met non-Jews frequently enough to know how to speak to them and deal with them. Later in Jerusalem, he was the leader of a multilingual community in a cosmopolitan city. It would be anachronistic to claim that James, unlike Jesus or Simon Peter, could have lived and worked in a kind of splendid isolation.[36] A striking example of James' own subtly bilingual approach can be found in his address at the so-called Apostolic Council in Jerusalem (Acts 15.6–29).[37] James, having listened to Peter's opening address and to the success story of Barnabas and Paul, does not insist on circumcising Gentile converts to Christianity, as some of the Pharisaic members of the community had done (Acts 15.5). 'We should not trouble the Gentiles who are turning to God,' he says, and merely suggests a number of dietary rules which would make sense to God-fearing Gentiles

(15.19–22); the council agrees unanimously. On the way to his conclusion, James quotes Jeremiah (12.15), Amos (9.11) and Isaiah (45.21).
Following Jewish custom, he does not quote them verbatim, but mod-
erately paraphrases and adapts these passages so as to drive home the
particular point he is trying to make. However, those present and also
the first bilingual readers of Acts would have noticed something immediately: the adapted quote from Amos is not taken from the Hebrew
Bible, but from the Septuagint. James elegantly demonstrates that he is
at home in both versions of the Tanakh, the Bible of all Jews.

The New Testament does not gloss over occasional conflicts of opinion. The Apostolic Council of Acts 15 is a good example of the
liveliness of such conflicts and the honest search for solutions. But it is
one of the myths about the New Testament that the cultural and linguistic attitudes and practices of the apostles also diverged. On the
contrary, it was because they each knew precisely what the other was
talking about and how the world around them was reacting to their
claims that they could debate these issues with different solutions in
mind. James was not an opponent of Paul's, and Paul is precise enough
(unlike some of his interpreters) to make this quite clear. The people
who threatened to drive a wedge between him and Peter, about the ritual legitimacy of common meals with Jewish Christians (still strictly
'kosher') and Gentile Christians (non-kosher) in Antioch (Galatians
2.12), had not been sent by James, they merely (and mistakenly)
claimed to act under his authority and to belong to his wider circle.[38]

The most remarkable aspect of the cosmopolitan, cross-cultural
strategy employed by the first Christians, including the leader of the
Jerusalem church, is of course the undeniable fact that all twenty-
seven texts of the New Testament were written and published in
Greek.[39] If the first Christians wanted their message to be read and
understood worldwide, by Jews and non-Jews alike, they simply had
no choice. Aramaic – let alone Hebrew – had become a minority language even among practising Jews throughout the Roman Empire and
beyond. The point is not that the first Christians chose Greek; this was
a missionary imperative. The point is that they knew what to use and
how to use it. And recent research has shown that this applied to James
in Jerusalem, as well. The Lord's brother knew both versions of the Old
Testament, the Hebrew as well as the Greek one, but the level of his
linguistic competence was also high enough for him to write a whole

letter in Greek, sent to the Jewish Christian communities in the Diaspora (James 1.1).[40]

But it was not only James' linguistic abilities which showed how much a part of the wider Jewish community he was. James' position as a whole must be understood from within Judaism. For example, the teachings of the Essenes, a rival 'messianic' movement, would have been known to him, as would the tenets of the Sadducees and Pharisees. His speech at the Apostolic Council includes allusions to Dead Sea Scrolls.[41] And this is not really surprising. We read in Acts 6.7 that members of the Essene community had become Christians.[42] Their writings had not been unknown to their fellow-Jews, and their hopes and expectations would obviously have been discussed among Jewish Christians, before and after the conversion of several Essene priests. Thus, by alluding to their writings, James is demonstrating to them that they have become valued members of the church in Jerusalem whose heritage is still valued. After all, that heritage was nothing to be ashamed of. Paul follows the same strategy. He insists, in his letter to the Philippians, that he is a Pharisee (3.5), and sees no reason to regret or deny this part of his Jewish identity. 'I am a Pharisee,' he declares in Acts 23.6, not 'I was a Pharisee.' This Jewish identity, personified by James and Paul, which was open-minded enough to accept Jesus as the Messiah and to envisage a mission to the whole world – even outside Judaism, as Jesus himself had undoubtedly demonstrated and wanted[43] – contrasts sharply with another form of 'cosmopolitan' lifestyle, the one preferred by the acting high priest at the time of Jesus, Joseph Bar Caiaphas.

Back in November 1990, in North Talpiot, a southern suburb of Jerusalem not far from the United Nations headquarters on the Hill of Evil Counsel, builders discovered unexpected traces from antiquity. They called in the Israel Antiquities Authority, and the archaeologist Zvi Greenhut found an extensive underground family tomb. Pottery and bones were scattered on the floor, and ossuaries which had been opened by tomb robbers. Since it was known that this area of Talpiot had been used for Jewish entombments, this new discovery was no surprise, but Greenhut investigated further and found a section largely undisturbed by robbers. This turned out to be the real sensation. Next to several decorated ossuaries without inscriptions, there were five with names. And two of them mentioned a certain Caiaphas.[44]

Greenhut consulted the leading epigrapher in Israel, Ronny Reich, who identified the name 'Qajfa' on one of them, and 'Jehosaf Bar Qajfa' on the other.[45] Father and son, or at least close relatives? Joseph Bar Caiaphas – this was the clue, for there is only one person of that name known from Jewish antiquity, the man who acted as high priest from AD 18–36. Josephus, who was born in the year of the high priest's removal from office by Vitellius, the Roman legate of Syria, refers to him as 'Joseph the Caiaphas' and 'Joseph called Caiaphas'.[46] The Gospels simply call him Caiaphas. Was the man whose name is inscribed on this second ossuary the high priest himself, or perhaps his son? The ossuary contained the bones of two infants, one child, one adult woman, a male adolescent of about eighteen, and those of a sixty-year-old man. It seems likely that the oldest person buried in this ossuary is the one whose name was inscribed on the outside. The other ossuary, with the simple inscription 'Qajfa', contained the bones of several people of a similar range of ages – but there was no sixty-year-old male.[47] In other words, this family tomb, which can be dated to the period of AD 41–48, contained an ossuary with the bones of one sixty-year-old man, and this increases the likelihood that 'Jehosaf Bar Qajfa' really is the high priest of Josephus and the Gospels.

In any case, and individual bones apart, this is the burial site of the Caiaphas family of New Testament times, and there was only one family of that name in those days. And there is a truly amazing inference from Zvi Greenhut's discovery. Caiaphas the high priest and those of his kind were Sadducees. But as we know from all existing sources (and have seen above), the Sadducees did not believe in the resurrection, let alone in a bodily one, with bones. Yet here they are, ceremoniously buried in beautifully decorated and hastily inscribed bone caskets, precisely according to the custom of those who did believe in just such a resurrection. In one of his great prophecies, Ezekiel had spoken of God's promise of a bodily resurrection (Ezekiel 37), and with unmistakable clarity, Isaiah had prophesied: 'Your dead shall live, their corpses shall rise' (Isaiah 26.19). Caiaphas and his family were unsure. Were these prophets right, after all, and their own Sadducean theology wrong? While playing the politically correct denier of the resurrection to the outside world, Caiaphas made sure that his body and those of his relatives were given secondary burials in ossuaries, so they would be ready to be raised in the last days – just in case.

Even more surprising, however, was a find in another ossuary nearby: the bone-casket of Miriam Berat Shimon, Miriam daughter of Simon. It contained her skull, and in the skull, between the jaws, a coin. It was well preserved and could be identified as a coin of Herod Agrippa I, with his name in Greek and dated to the sixth year of his reign, AD 42/3 in modern chronology. This was the Agrippa who executed James, the brother of John, and imprisoned Peter, and whose cruel death in AD 44 was reported by Luke and Josephus.[48] Both authors describe Agrippa I as a blasphemer and agree that he met a deserved end. But how did one of the coins minted under his reign find its way into the mouth of Miriam? Not by accident, of course. It was a time-honoured pagan custom to place a coin in the mouth – under the tongue or between the teeth – of a deceased person. This way, the bereaved family paid Charon, the ferryman, who ferried the dead (or rather the shades) across the River Styx into Hades.[49] This was the realm where the dead rested, inaccessible to the living, and not all myths about it describe the place as frightening. Two variations of the theme of Hades even became popular operas, Christoph Willibald Gluck's *Orfeo ed Euridice* (1762) and Jacques Offenbach's *Orphée aux enfers* (1858). Charon himself may have been envisaged as a frightening sight – the name means 'he with the glittering eyes'. The pagan custom of paying the *naūlon* or *porthmēnion*, Charon's fare, seems to have been taken up by Jews. Not far from Jericho, the archaeologist Rachel Hachlili found a necropolis with two Jewish sarcophagi – i.e. coffins used for the first burial before the transferral to ossuaries – and in one of them, the skull of a woman contained a coin of Herod Archaelaus (AD 4–6), a son of Herod the Great. Nearby, Hachlili found an ossuary with a skull and two coins of Herod Agrippa I in it.[50] Non-Jews in the Holy Land also paid Charon; in the so-called Tomb of Jason, there were so many coins that they could have been intended as a kind of pocket money for life in Hades.[51] Only a few ossuaries with coins have been found so far, and thus one cannot tell how widespread the custom may have been among multicultural Jews. The one family, however, where no one would have expected it was the family of the high priest, the official guardian of the Law and its orthodox observance. But we now know that the Caiaphas family willingly broke the Second Commandment (Exodus 20.1–5), honouring the pagan myth of Charon and the god who personified the Underworld, Hades.

Josephus, himself of priestly descent and a Pharisee, knew about the popularity of pagan cults among many of his fellow Jews. When Agrippa I died in AD 44, he writes that the citizens of Caesarea and Samaria joyfully celebrated the event in the streets by pouring out libations to Charon.[52] After all, even in the regions of Galilee, Samaria and Judaea, not all Jews were observant in those days. They borrowed from different traditions, from the Egyptians, from the Greeks, from the Romans, and from others. It was a kind of socio-religious self-service shop, and it was left to the priests, the scribes, the Sadducees, the Pharisees and the ultra-orthodox Essenes to teach and write about the Torah, God's law, and its abiding importance for their times. So it was not only in the eyes of Jesus that too many of them failed much too often. But it was particularly galling to hear the Sadducees denying biblical prophecy by refusing to teach the physical resurrection, that signal event of hope and reconciliation for the people of Israel. Caiaphas accused Jesus of blasphemy and tore his clothes in a dramatic gesture (Matthew 26.65). But now we know that it was actually Caiaphas, whose family stooped to pagan worship behind closed doors, who was the real blasphemer, a syncretist whose cronies had been unmasked by the pious Jew Jesus: 'Woe to you scribes and Pharisees, hypocrites! For you are like whitewashed tombs, which on the outside look beautiful, but inside they are full of the bones of the dead and of all kinds of filth. So you also on the outside look righteous to others, but inside you are full of hypocrisy and lawlessness' (Matthew 23.27–8).

As the archaeological discovery in North Talpiot has shown, Caiaphas' negative image is not an 'anti-Jewish' invention by the Gospel authors. Apart from his role in the trial and crucifixion of Jesus, he also collaborated with the Roman occupying power to the disadvantage of the people – it was he, as the acting high priest, who let Pilate take money from the treasury of the Temple, to fund an aqueduct into Jerusalem, a controversial action which caused riots brutally quelled by Pilate's soldiers.[53] Indirectly at least, Caiaphas had blood on his hands. Caiaphas also invited vendors into the Temple precincts, offending orthodox Jews like Jesus and Simeon ben Gamaliel.[54] The Roman legate Vitellius later put an end to many of these practices, not least the financial exploitation of the population which the high priest and the prefect had apparently engineered in tandem – it was the first measure he took after removing both Caiaphas and Pilate from office in AD 37.[55]

When the Talmud condemns the high priests and their kind with a 'Woe', the reason was not any action against Jesus, which, after all, followed due legal procedures and left the responsibility entirely and exclusively in the hands of the Roman prefect, but the corruptibility and connivance with the occupying authorities which had harmed the Jewish people.[56] Such assessments are based on Talmudic sources and have nothing to do with anti-Semitic or anti-Jewish tendencies.

The discovery of the Caiaphas family tomb, with Miriam's coin and their beautiful ossuaries, contributes to our understanding of the close-knit network of cultural links in the Roman Empire at the time of Jesus. Throughout this chapter, we have seen that the world of Jesus and his contemporaries was anything but a secluded corner of the empire, in the back of beyond. Jews and non-Jews alike had opportunities to live multicultural lives, well connected with other centres of the empire, from Alexandria via Antioch to Athens and Rome. It is what they did and how they did it which often enough caused the wrath of Jesus, not his surprise that they were able to do it at all.

6 Back to the Sources: Bookshops, Libraries and Messengers

'Well, Father Sebastian said to answer all your questions but there is not much I can tell you about the papyrus. You probably know as much as I do. It was certainly given to Miss Arbuthnot in 1887 by her brother and he was certainly capable of forging it or having it forged. He was a man fond of practical jokes and this would have appealed to him. He was a fervent atheist. Can an atheist be fervent? Anyway, he was anti-religion.'

'What is the papyrus exactly?'

'It purports to be a communication from Pontius Pilate to an officer of the guard regarding the removal of a certain body.'

P. D. James, *Death in Holy Orders*

When you come, bring the cloak that I left with Carpus at Troas, also the books, and above all the parchments.

2 Timothy 4.13

An ancient travelling library

So, from his childhood to the cross and the empty tomb, Jesus was part of a cosmopolitan world. It was a world which left us a rich legacy of artefacts. Most of them, however, would remain mute without the inscriptions and, above all, the manuscripts. Pliny the Elder – Gaius Plinius Secundus – summed it up in his *Natural History*, a magisterial 37-volume encyclopaedia of everything the ancients knew about the natural world, which he left unfinished when he died inhaling fumes during a rescue attempt after the eruption of Vesuvius on 24 August AD 79. Commenting on the popularity of papyrus, he wrote: 'Everywhere, the use of the material on which the immortality of mankind rests was disseminated.'[1] Discoveries from antiquity have shown that papyrus from Egypt was in use as writing material as early as the fourteenth century BC. The writer of the book of Job knew about it: 'Can the papyrus grow up without marsh? Can the reed grass grow without water?' (Job 8.11)

The priest mentioned in Numbers 5.23 uses a papyrus: 'Then the priest shall put these curses in writing, and *wash them off* into the water of bitterness.' The Bible is full of direct references to writing on papyrus, parchment or leather – all of these materials were used for scrolls or single leaves. Here is an example from the New Testament: 'I had much to write to you; however, I did not want to do it with papyrus and black ink, but I hope to come to you and speak with you personally, so that our joy may be complete' (2 John 12). In fact, the number of references to writing and writing materials in the Bible, from the days of Moses to the final pages of Revelation, is impressive enough:

Exodus 24.6–7, 34.1	36.16–18	Galatians 6.11
Numbers 5.23	Ezekiel 2.9–10, 4.1,	Colossians 4.16–18
1 Kings 21.8	9.2, 37.16–17	2 Thessalonians 2.2,
Job 8.11, 19.23–4,	Habakkuk 2.2–3	3.17
31.35	Luke 1.63, 4.16–17	2 Timothy 4.13
Psalm 45.2	John 8.6, 19.19–20	1 Peter 5.12
Isaiah 34.4	Acts 15.22–3	2 John 12
Jeremiah 17.1,	Romans 16.22	3 John 13
32.13–14,	1 Corinthians 16.21	Revelation 5.1, 6.14

The New Testament passages are particularly instructive; the writers used precise terminology, and their asides can be read as an introduction to reading and writing habits in the Greek-speaking regions of the Roman Empire. In Luke 1.63, Zechariah, the father of John, the Baptist-to-be, cannot tell his family and relatives the name of the newborn son, since he is temporarily mute. So they give him a writing tablet. As noted previously, the Greek word in Luke's Gospel is *pinakidion*, and this is the technical term for a writing tablet with a wax surface, used for short notes and messages, and often for school exercises. The metal or wooden stylus had a broad, flat end which was used to erase the text. Many such styli and writing tablets, some even with wax and writing, have been found and are displayed in numerous museums. As an assistant priest (Luke 1.5–9), Zechariah knew how to write. When he wrote, 'all of them were amazed' (Luke 1.63) – not because he was able to write on a *pinakidion*, but because he chose a name they had not expected, chosen by the angel (Luke 1.13) rather than from family tradition.

In Luke 4.16–17, it is not only evident that Jesus could read Hebrew and knew how to handle a scroll; the incident also reveals the technicalities of reading from a biblical book in a synagogue. Today, only the Torah or Pentateuch, that is the five books of Moses, and the book of Esther are read from scrolls in the synagogues; all the others are ordinary printed books. But in those days, the psalms, the prophets and the other writings were all read from scrolls. After the reading from the Torah, a set portion from another book was read by a male member of the congregation, or an honoured guest who had to be over thirteen years old, and, needless to say, a circumcised Jew. This reading was called the 'Haftara' – literally the 'conclusion' or 'completion'. Thus, when Jesus was asked to read the Haftara, it was first of all an honour, since he no longer lived in Nazareth and was not a member of the congregation. And second, he did not choose the text. It was the set text for that day – a fact which makes the prophetic fire which Jesus kindles from these lines all the more remarkable. A member of the synagogue told Jesus what the passage was and gave him the scroll of Isaiah. The person who read the Haftara from Isaiah on a previous day had rolled the scroll together from both ends, so that Jesus did not have to unroll the whole scroll from the beginning. However, since biblical scrolls in those days did not have chapter and verse divisions, a passage was usually identified by its first words or sentence, and this is what Jesus had to find before he could begin to read Isaiah 61.1–2.[2] Afterwards, he would have rolled both sides of the scroll back together again, to meet in the middle, with the greater part of the roll on the right-hand side and a smaller one – only five 'chapters' remained – on the left.

In John 8.6, 'Jesus bent down and wrote with his finger on the ground'. The Greek text is unambiguous: he did not doodle, he really wrote. In other words, even though the practice of writing on the ground was certainly unusual, it was a word or perhaps even the recognizable beginning of a prophetic teaching. Some scholars have suggested Exodus 23.7 ('Have nothing to do with a false charge'). We do not know, but John 8.6 adds to our picture of Jesus the literate man: he not only read biblical Hebrew at the synagogue, but was able to write as well.

John 19.19–20 is the most detailed of the four Gospel accounts of Pilate's inscription on the cross of Jesus. As we saw in Chapter 5, John's accuracy is remarkable. And classical historians use his report (together with those in Matthew 27.37, Mark 15.26 and Luke 23.38) as one of the few surviving examples of the Roman practice of proclaiming the reason for the punishment of a condemned person publicly on a headboard, a *titulus* in Latin or *titlos* in Greek.[3] The fragment of the *titulus* at Santa Croce in Gerusalemme, a church built above Empress Helena's early fourth-century palace, the Sessorianum in Rome, explains why the text could be read easily by visitors and pilgrims entering and leaving the city (John 19.20). It was a typical *tabula dealbata*, a whitened piece of wood, with incised letters filled in with red or reddish-black colouring, measuring *c.* 60 centimetres by 21 centimetres.[4] Pilate's headboard, proclaiming the reason for the punishment, followed an official formula. Such standard forms of communication often extended to stylized beginnings and endings of letters, and the letter sent by the 'Apostolic Council' in Jerusalem to communities in Antioch and beyond (Acts 15.22–3) is another remarkable example of this practice.

Further passages in the New Testament illuminate scribal habits and the distribution of roles between the actual author of a text and his trusted secretary – habits common throughout the Roman Empire. In Romans 16.22, Tertius sends his own greetings first, as the one who wrote the letter. This implies that he was more than a mere scribe. Paul had given him an important task: he may have written from dictation, probably in shorthand, and was responsible for the edited, completed scroll of the letter.[5] At the end of 1 Corinthians (16.21), written with a scribal assistant who was important enough to be mentioned by name (Sosthenes, 1.1), Paul signs the letter with his own hand. It follows that the preceding leaves of the scroll were not in his handwriting. The same happens in Galatians, a letter where no co-author or scribe is mentioned but which was evidently not written by Paul until 6.11. 'See what large letters I use when I write in my own hand,' Paul exclaims, and we are led to assume that the apostle concludes the letter, another eight verses, himself.

The reference to the 'large letters' highlights another aspect of ancient writing. A letter, as a personal document, was written in a cursive style, and the more professional the scribe, the more elegant and compact this cursive style would have been. But Paul the elitist Pharisee was used to dictating his letters and furthermore, multilingual as he was, he was accustomed to the scrolls of the Hebrew and Greek 'Old Testament', of the Greek philosophers, poets and dramatists which were written in uncials, the upright writing style used for literature and documents. After the scribe's cursive chapters, he concludes Galatians with his own authoritative, documentary style, in capital letters, the classical uncials. Paul's habit of authorizing letters with his own signature can also be found in Colossians 4.16–18 and 2 Thessalonians 3.17. The signature in 2 Thessalonians follows a strict rebuttal of pseudepigraphy, that is of people claiming to write in Paul's name and with his authority (2.2). It is one of the persistent myths of New Testament scholarship that the early Church did not mind if a letter was not written by the apostle whose name it carried, and that 'epistolary pseudepigraphy' – the habit of publishing letters under another name – may have been an acceptable way of honouring the apostle. Amusingly, many scholars have relegated Colossians, with its apostolic signature, to the pile of letters allegedly not written by Paul. 2 Thessalonians 2.2 and 3.17 are among the explicit passages in early Christian literature which refute this scholarly myth-making; others went further, and a forger of an apostolic document, a pseudepigrapher, could be excommunicated.[6] Peter, also under suspicion of not having written his two letters, refers to his secretary Silvanus in 1 Peter 5.12. Silvanus is the Silas/Silvanus of Acts 15.22, 2 Corinthians 1.19, 1 Thessalonians 1.1, and 2 Thessalonians 1.1, and it seems that he was not only a skilled writer, but also a communicator and a teacher in his own right. In fact, a good secretary was more like a personal assistant or aide-de-camp, authorized to act on behalf of his employer even in his absence. Silas/Silvanus, a Roman citizen (Acts 16.37–9) who worked both for Paul and for Peter, is one of the eminent examples of this profession in classical literature.

Brief, personal letters were often written by the correspondents themselves. Thousands of such personal messages have survived in the papyrus collections of Oxford, Cambridge, London, Vienna, Berlin, Milan, and Paris. In the New Testament, the only letter of Paul short and personal enough to 'qualify' is the letter to Philemon, but he did not write it quite on his own: Timothy was his assistant or co-author. Thus, we are left with two of the Johannine letters, and both add to the collection of writing vocabulary we have encountered so far. First, consider 2 John 12: 'Although I have much to write to you, I would rather not use paper and ink; instead I hope to come to you and talk with you face to face, so that our joy may be complete'. 'Paper', here and in some other translations, is of course an anachronism – invented probably in China, it was only introduced to the Middle East and Europe in the early eleventh century. The Greek word is *chartēs*, and technically,

this means a leaf of papyrus. John means what he says: his second letter was short enough to fit on one papyrus leaf. Occasionally, *chartēs*
meant a complete scroll. If there was a danger of confusion, writers
would use *chartion* for the leaf, and *chartēs* for the scroll. The best
modern translation of 2 John 2.12 would be something like 'with
papyrus and ink'. The second technical term is *melan*, which means ink,
a word derived from *melas*, 'black' or 'very dark'. In those days, the
standard mixture for the production of ink was soot, gum arabic and
water, and it is a very durable concoction, as demonstrated by the many
papyri which have survived under the protective conditions of the
Egyptian desert or the Dead Sea.

John writes about ink again in his third letter, 3 John 13, another very
short epistle for a single sheet or leaf, and he adds another useful word,
kalamos, which means 'reed' and, more specifically, a reed-pen as writing instrument. In Greek literature, one of the best-known references to
this is Psalm 45.1 in the Septuagint (third/second century BC): 'My
tongue is the reed-pen of a shorthand writer'.[7] Those writing imple-
ments were like the precursors of modern fountain-pen tips, with a
sharp end, and split at the tip. Demanding writers had their favourite
suppliers: Pliny the Elder preferred reed-pens from Cnidus in south-
west Asia Minor and from Armenia; Martial, a younger contemporary
of the apostles (*c.* AD 40–102), liked reeds from Egypt.[8]

The most fascinating of all New Testament passages about writing
and communication, however, is 2 Timothy 4.13. It is important enough
for papyrologists and classical philologists to quote in textbooks on
papyrology and the textual tradition of the classics. The reason is simple
enough, though it is not obvious from a standard English translation,
where we find, for example: 'When you come, bring the cloak that I left
with Carpus at Troas, also the books, and above all the parchments'
(NRSV). Read in isolation like this, the verse does not make much
sense. What cloak, what books, what parchments, and why in this context and order? Papyrologists have always noted that the last word,
translated here as 'parchments', is in Greek *membranas*. And they have
ascertained that it is originally a Latin word, transcribed into Greek as a
technical term, and that it means parchment 'notebooks'. These notebooks were made from single leaves, loosely held together by leather
bands. In the Latin-speaking West, they had been introduced by Julius
Caesar.[9] The poet Horace (65–8 BC) explains that notebooks made from

parchment increasingly replaced those made from combined single wax-tablets.[10] In addition to these pre-Christian references, there is one from a Latin author who was an exact contemporary of Paul's, the poet and satirist Persius (AD 34–62). He mentions a student with a hangover who hastily bundles together his belongings, among them a parchment note-book.[11] In any case, Paul apparently had a number of such books containing his notes and drafts of his letters, and therefore it was essential for him to retrieve them. And since he writes about them in Greek, his reference makes him the first and only Greek author of the first century to mention parchment notebooks.[12] In Jewish Christian circles, this practice – which Paul had of course begun before he mentions it in 2 Timothy 4.13 – made him an innovator. As we shall see in a moment, the Pauline notebooks may well have been a first step towards the introduction of a new practical book-format, the codex. And since 2 Timothy was written during Paul's second imprisonment in Rome, it may be assumed that he had been introduced to the format, and to the Latin term which he then turned into Greek, even before he returned to the very city where the 'loose-leaf' notebook had been introduced by Julius Caesar.

The second Greek technical term in 2 Timothy 4.13 is *biblia*, which literally means 'books' and is the root of our modern word 'Bible'. In Paul's day, however, it meant 'scrolls'. Within the New Testament, its usage is explained by two passages in Revelation: 'Then I saw in the right hand of the one seated on the throne a scroll [Greek *biblion*], written in the inside and on the back, sealed with seven seals' (5.1), and 'The sky vanished like a scroll (*biblion*) rolling itself up' (6.14). Paul does not tell Timothy what kind of scrolls he had left behind. They may have been scrolls of 'Old Testament' writings, or copies of his own letters, or of a Gospel like Mark's or Luke's, or of some Gentile Greek author he had read, like Aeschylus, Euripides, Aratus, Callimachus or Menander. But we do know that his collection of texts consisted of such scrolls, and of his own notebooks. It is obvious enough that he needed them for his teaching and his own writings, and why. But why did he need his cloak? This is the real enigma in this sentence, and the solution sheds light on another neglected aspect of the cosmopolitan world in which Jesus and his followers lived and worked.

Historically speaking, his situation was typical enough: here was a traveller – in Paul's case a prisoner – taken by ship to Rome, journeying from port to port and waiting for the ideal weather. Particularly during the late autumn, this was a question of patience and very sudden decisions. And we know from the context of 2 Timothy 4.13 that Paul left Troas in late autumn: 'Do your best to come before winter' (4.21). One such day, probably at dawn, the captain of the ship decided that the conditions were good and everyone had to embark immediately. Paul, not entirely free in his movements anyway, is hurried along and leaves his possessions behind. As soon as he gets a chance, he writes and asks for them to be sent to him. This type of cloak, a *phailonēs* in Greek, was a one-piece wrap of rough wool, with an opening in the middle for the head. Useful as it was in a cold climate, it was of no value at all compared to the scrolls and the notebooks. His hosts and friends in Rome and indeed anywhere else on his route could have given him more than one immediately. Forced to take a closer look, one can see what the Greek word *phailonēs* really means. As the first word in the list, it refers to the receptacle, the covering cloak used to keep and transport scrolls. Paul simply asks for his complete set of documents, contained in the cloak or wrapper that always covered and protected them for transport. Receptacle, scrolls and notebooks are a unity in 2 Timothy 4.13, and the most appropriate translation would be, 'When you come, bring the wrapper that I left with Carpus at Troas, also the scrolls, and above all the parchment notebooks.'[13] Like *membrana*, *phailonēs* was originally a Latin word, *paenula*. In Latin, it also means 'cloak', but Paul's usage was not unknown at the time – there is at least one other case, in Latin literature, during the late Pauline period, where it was used to describe a wrapping cover: Martial's epigrams.[14]

Generally speaking, in order to save time, Paul could actually have dispatched some of his shorter letters straight from the notebook, or some of his notebooks could have circulated as study material among his students in Rome and elsewhere. His colleagues, followers and scribes took things one step further. From then on, it was easy enough for Christians to see that the notebook format was a model capable of development. Fold a large sheet of papyrus – or parchment – several times, and place these folded sheets on top of each other, then bind them together and cut the pages open: the result was a handy but sizeable 'notebook' which could now be used for long literary and documentary texts, like the notebook with writing on both sides. Paul's letters, or eventually the five scrolls of the Gospels and Acts, could be published as one single, handy codex.[15] At roughly the same time, in the early eighties of the first century, the Roman poet Martial propagated the parchment and papyrus 'paperback' (or 'pocket-size') codex. The great classics, he wrote – authors like Homer, Virgil, Ovid (and for good measure, he added his own name) – should be read in the practical codex rather than in the enormous scrolls which take up so much space on journeys. In one of his poems, his second epigram, he even mentions the name of his publisher, Secundus, and the address of his shop at the market of Pallas Athene in Rome. In other words, when the first Christian codices were published, Roman readers would not regard them as odd, obscure and somewhat sectarian, but novel, daring, and very much at the forefront of technical development. It was a great chance for the Christian writings to get noticed.

But it was precisely the popularity of the codex among Christians which eventually made the old guard of Gentile Roman bookworms turn away from it. In the mid-second century, they returned to the time-honoured scroll, and it was left mainly to the Christians to cultivate the codex, until Emperor Constantine finally initiated its more general use for all types of literature. From the second century, fourteen fragmentary codices have survived, two on parchment, and twelve on papyrus. By the end of the fourth century, 90.5 per cent of all manuscripts which have survived were written in the form of papyrus or parchment codices. The scroll, common to the Jews, the first generation of Christian scribes and authors, and to everyone writing in Greek and Latin, was an undeniable link between the cultures. The development of the codex from the notebooks of Latin politicians and poets, and from Paul's practical needs, on the other hand, is an example of the constant cross-fertilization of ideas between Christianity and its Gentile environment in the early decades of the Church. Jews, Greeks and Romans used the same writing materials, the same ink, the same types of reed-pen and stylus, and, to begin with at least, the same format: the scroll with writing on the inside. Occasional exceptions proved the 'rule': the marked preference for leather, rather than the refined parchment which could of course also have been produced, like leather, from kosher animals, was a hallmark of the Dead Sea Scrolls. Only some twenty-five papyrus fragments were found in the caves, among thousands of leather scraps.

Being on the market

The early production of the Gospels or Paul's letters, in Greek, on scrolls, was a missionary priority. But the early literary activities of the first Christians were not limited to the twenty-seven texts which finally made it into the authoritative canon of the New Testament as we still have it today. Long before pseudo-Christian writings were published with obscure teachings like the so-called Gospels of Peter and of Thomas, mid- to late-second-century oddities which appear to titillate members of the 'Jesus Seminar' and other outsiders, but which otherwise are of merely church-historical interest, committed Christians had written and distributed their own thoughts about Jesus and the early Church. Letters such as the one by Clement of Rome to the church in Corinth, written in *c.* AD 69, or, as others think, in AD 98, but undoubtedly before the end of the first century, were both popular and orthodox in their teaching, and they were copied often enough to survive the first centuries. Clement's first letter was included in one of the most important biblical codices, the early-fifth-century Codex Alexandrinus. The *Letter of Barnabas* and the *Shepherd of Hermas* were included in the oldest and most famous Greek codex of the whole Bible, the Codex Sinaiticus of *c.* AD 330. (Both codices can be seen in the British Library.) Early as these writings are, they post-date the canonical Gospels and belong to the fast-growing collection of literature which individual Christians, communities and eventually heretics of all sorts produced for a market which demanded exciting news about the life and teachings of Jesus. Closer to the time of Jesus, local witnesses had written down what they had heard and seen, and Luke refers to such sources in the prologue to his Gospel: 'Many have undertaken to draw up an account of the things which have been fulfilled among us' (Luke 1.1).[16] None of these early, pre-Gospel sources has survived, either in Aramaic or in Greek. What we can read today, outside the New Testament, are later documents, from *1 Clement* and the so-called 'Apostolic Fathers' to the mass of pseudo-Gospels collected in editions of 'New Testament Apocrypha'.

The pseudo-Gospels in particular are a salutary reminder of the novelistic, occasionally heretical, but sometimes also pious third stage of Christian literature, which was far removed from the sober, down-to-earth approach of the historical writings contained in the New Testament. Read these texts, and you will appreciate once more the outstanding quality of the four Gospels and the other canonical texts. With only a little effort, everyone can form their own opinion. These writings or their extant fragments are not hidden in secret archives of churches like skeletons in cupboards; they have all been edited and translated.

But there is yet another group of early Christian documents which do not belong to any of these categories: potsherds (*ostraca*) with passages from the New Testament, for example, and private correspondence between Christians. They are the unknown treasures of Christian beginnings. Some of them concern simple matters of daily life, such as taxes, invitations and wine cellars; others record unpleasant attitudes among non-Christian inhabitants of one's village or town. They were not written to teach and inform, like the letters of the New Testament and the apostolic writers, but to invite to a meeting, or to acknowledge a delivery of goods; they included greetings for the brethren, invocations of God, even Christian symbols like the cross or the Chi-Rho. They are the everyday, even mundane side of early Christian literature.

They also tell us that as late as AD 270, Christian children in Egypt could still be given names like 'Hierakammon' or 'Asklepios', the names of pagan gods (as noted earlier, Asklepios was the Greek god of medical arts; Hierakammon was the holy Ammon, the highest-ranking Egyptian god, on a par with the Greek Zeus).[17] Was early Egyptian Christianity corrupted by the old, unforgotten pagan habits? Or was this just a reflection of cultural traditions, continued by devout Christians as an integral part of their 'tribal' affiliations, with no tangible influence on their religious way of life?[18] Our first surprise at the plainly non-Christian, utterly pagan names of those two correspondents in Egypt subsides if we remember that two of the twelve disciples, both devout Jews, had pagan, Greek, non-Jewish names: Andrew ('the manly one') and Philip ('the friend of horses').

New light on such matters has been shed by the recent re-evaluation of the earliest non-canonical Christian letter ever discovered. Dated to the late first century, to a time when some members of the apostolic generation (like John) and many who had met Jesus and the disciples were still alive, the Papyrus P.Oxyr. 3057 from the upper Egyptian town of Oxyrhynchus was written by Ammonios to his brother Apollonios, son of Apollos. The names could hardly be more pagan. 'Ammonios' is derived from the Egyptian god Ammon, and 'Apollonios', with his father Apollos – also the personal name of an eminent first-generation Jewish Christian (Acts 18.24–8, 19.1; 1 Corinthians 3.4–6, etc.) – from the Greek god Apollo. Perhaps their parents were not Christians, but even the name of the scribe to whom the letter was dictated, Leonas, is Greek and pagan – as was that of the

Roman citizen and Christian scribe Silas/Silvanus who wrote for Peter and Paul some thirty years earlier. The letter is very personal: it begins with thanks for the sending of cloaks and sheets for papyrus scrolls (probably with the scrolls inside). It resolves a misunderstanding and hopes that all discord among brethren can be avoided, and it ends with the heartfelt wish that the recipient may remain calm in troubled times. Nothing exciting, in other words: no new heights of Christian thought, but the down-to-earth reality of everyday life in early Christianity. It is certainly not as devout in its introductory and con- cluding words as the apostolic letters: 'Ammonios greets his brother Apollonios. I have received the letter . . .' is how it begins; and at the end, we read: 'I, Leonas, greet you, O master, you and all yours. Remain well, O most honourable one.'[19] One gets the impression that people like Hierakammon, Asklepios, Ammonios and Apollonios did not discuss matters of faith in their everyday correspondence and led their daily lives like everyone else – and in a way, that makes this first- century letter so illuminating. Christianity, after all, did not exist in a cultural vacuum. These people, while practising their faith with all due neighbourly love and regular worship, left theology and doctrinal mat- ters to the teachers of the faith, much like most Christians would do today, avoiding the temptation to emulate an official letter written by their diocesan bishop in their private correspondence. After all, these were all real people, real Christians with hopes and anxieties.

The private side of multilingual, cross-cultural Christianity in New Testament times is as fascinating as the public one, of libraries, book- shops and other means of reaching readers. And again, the traditions behind these instruments of communication and learning were known to Jews and Christians as much as to other educated people in those societies. In the early third century BC, Demetrius of Phaleron, the first director of the world-famous library of Alexandria (he lived from *c.* 354 to *c.* 283 BC) wrote to King Ptolemy I: 'It is necessary that the books of the Jewish Law find their place in your library, in a correct translation.' This, according to a tradition told in the so-called 'Letter of Aristeas', which was written in the late third or early second century BC, gave rise to the first complete translation of the Hebrew Bible into Greek, later to be called the 'Septuagint', which has been quoted more than once in this book.[20] The 'Letter of Aristeas' and the traditions behind it are hotly disputed by modern scholars. But one thing is certain. When Philo of Alexandria (*c.* 30 BC–*c.* AD 50) appeared on the scene, he had access to the complete Jewish Bible in Greek, and to the wealth of 'pagan' Greek literature which he, who knew no Hebrew, used widely and to great effect. The synagogues of Alexandria would have possessed the biblical scrolls in Hebrew and Greek, but for proper academic study and writing, all Philo had to do was to enter the public library with its two sections, the Museion and the overflow storage shelves in the Serapaion with their estimated 530,800 to 700,000 scrolls, apply for a reader's ticket and withdraw what he needed.[21] The resources of the library of Alexandria were instrumental in the development of Jewish thought in Greek during the two or three centuries before the first Christian writings were published – and we should remember that these writings, too, were written by Jews, and in Greek.

Philo, the Jew who made the most of the Library of Alexandria, whose writings were preserved, copied and passed on by Christians rather than by orthodox Jews from late antiquity through the Middle Ages to the first printed copies, was one of those Jews who showed to Christians – both of Jewish and of Gentile origin – that it was possible to combine Greek classical knowledge with the message of the five books of Moses, the Torah, and indeed of the whole Jewish Bible, without belittling or denying the veracity of the Jewish heritage. And the strategy of early Christianity, from Peter and Paul to the outstanding Christian philosophers of the second and third centuries, was clear enough: try to convince the Greeks and the Romans that the Judaeo-Christian message was attractive to people trained in classical thought. Paul tried this in Athens, when he addressed the philosophers of the Areopagus and began by quoting the popular philosopher Aratus (Acts 17.28; Aratus, *Phainomena* 5). And as we saw above, this was the same apostle who quoted from a play by Euripides and who was capable of rendering a verse from Aeschylus in perfect Greek. Paul may have acquired his knowledge of Greek literature in Tarsus, a city with a renowned library. But the first outstanding Christian masters of Greek literature were two men who had studied at Alexandria, with immediate access to its library, magnificently rebuilt as it was by then, after the fire of 48 BC: Clement of Alexandria and Origen.

Clement (*c.* AD 150–*c.* AD 216), born in Athens, studied under Pantaenus at the catechetical school in Alexandria, the Didascaleion with its own well-endowed library. One of his own most influential books was the so-called *Protrepticus*, an analysis of Greek mysteries from a Christian perspective. It was a book written not for Christians, but for educated 'pagan' thinkers, people who like Clement himself had read the religious and philosophical scrolls in the library of Alexandria, and indeed elsewhere. And it remains an outstanding example of almost encyclopaedic knowledge of non-Jewish and non-Christian literature combined with a profound understanding of classical Jewish texts and the New Testament. Clement's successor was a man who had sat at his and Pantaenus' feet: Origen, born in Alexandria in *c.* AD 184. He was one of the virtuosi of Greek literature and philology, and even non-Christians came to study under him, first at Alexandria and later at Caesarea Maritima – the Caesarea where Peter had converted a Roman centurion and his household (Acts 10), where Philip the Evangelist had settled (Acts 21.9) and where Paul had been imprisoned (Acts 23.35). Here, he established the first Christian library, employed stenographers, copyists, and calligraphers, and compiled a collection of 30,000 scrolls of Christian, Jewish, Greek and Roman literature. Among many theological works, one of his philosophical books has survived complete: *Against Celsus*, a brilliant refutation of a widely known polemic against Christianity. Like Clement before him, Origen demonstrated that Greek thinkers can be beaten at their own game, and like Clement, his approach was constructive rather than destructive. Intelligent, open-minded readers were meant to understand that the Christian faith was accessible to thinking people. Faith in Christ and in the God of the Bible did not presuppose the abandonment of one's intellectual capabilities – quite the contrary. Remember that all this was achieved while Christianity was a religion rejected, often despised and occasionally persecuted by Roman officialdom. Origen himself had been forced to leave Alexandria during Emperor Caracalla's massacre of local Christians in AD 215 and was tortured repeatedly in the Decian persecution of 250–1.

After Origen's death in 252, his successor Pamphilius extended the collection, and when Eusebius of Caesarea (*c.* 260–339) took over, the famous church historian and trusted adviser of the first Christian Emperor, Constantine, this Christian library of cross-cultural learning had become famous throughout the Roman Empire. Eusebius owed a decisive debt to Origen, his library and his strategic concept when, soon after AD 313, he wrote his *Praeparatio Evangelica*, a *Preparation for the Gospel* which showed that pagan philosophy was basically nothing but a step (albeit an important step) towards the full truth revealed in Christ. In the Latin-speaking West, in Rome, the Christian lawyer Minucius Felix had employed similar tactics as early as *c.* AD 150, almost half a century before the more famous Tertullian, when he used Cicero and other thinkers in his dialogue *Octavius*.[22] In the dialogue, a non-Christian and a Christian debate the truthfulness of the Christian faith, and in a final comment Minucius praises the Christian, Octavius Ianuarius, because he had succeeded in 'parrying spiteful critics with their own weapons, with the arrows of philosophers, and had shown the truth to be so simple as well as so attractive'.[23]

It is obvious that the first Christians studied their own Jewish source-book, the one we have come to call the Old Testament. They also read texts which were not included in the Hebrew canon, like *Enoch* (Jude 14), the *Apocalypse of Elijah* (1 Corinthians 2.9), and *Baruch* (= *Letter of Jeremiah*; 1 John 5.21). They apparently knew of the Greek classics even in New Testament times and made extensive use of them, and long before Christianity became a legitimate religion (a *religio licita*) in the Roman Empire, they also read and quoted the Latin classics. Libraries played an important part in their education and gave them their intellectual equipment, from Tarsus via Alexandria to Caesarea. Every major city had a study library in those days.[24] But the Christians, just like the Jews, always had their own synagogal and community libraries as well. Acts 17.10–11 gives a prime example: 'That very night the believers sent Paul and Silas off to Beroea; and when they arrived, they went to the Jewish synagogue. These Jews were more receptive than those in Thessalonica, for they welcomed the message very eagerly and examined the scriptures every day to see whether these things were so.' How could these Jews in Beroea examine the scriptures? As far as we can tell, every synagogue had a library. First, there was the Torah, the five books of Moses. It was kept in the *Aaron ha-Kodesh*, the shrine for the Torah scrolls in the synagogue, which was opened only when the congregation met to hear the set portion on the eve of the Sabbath, during the Sabbath services, and on the holy days of the Jewish year. A second set of the Torah scrolls was usually kept in the library, so that members of the community, led by the rabbi or another qualified person, could study the Law at other times. And as we saw above, the scrolls of the Law were important enough to be made accessible in the Museion, in the great library of Alexandria.

The synagogal libraries would have contained the scrolls of the Haftara, the biblical books read during the service to aid exposition of the portion of the Torah, and at least one scroll of the Psalms. And there were also many other texts in these libraries, including those popular but non-canonical writings like *Enoch* and *Baruch*. The Qumran library of the Essenes may be our only surviving example of a Jewish library of the Second Temple period, but it goes without saying that other communities were as interested in the different genres of Jewish literature as the Essenes. Collecting new texts which could help them understand the fulfilment of prophecy and the dawning of the messianic age was a librarian's task. Nicholas Orme, Professor of History at Exeter University, recently asked a pertinent question: if none of the Gospels had been published before the Apostle Paul wrote his letters, how could he afford to say so little about the life and the sayings of Jesus?[25] This is an historian's question – most New Testament scholars, ensconced in their world of post-Pauline Gospels, would not even understand what he is saying.[26] With Orme's searching question in mind, we may wonder if the library of the synagogue at Beroea did not contain a copy of an early Christian writing. Paul and Silas' mission to Beroea should be dated to AD 47/8. By then, Mark's Gospel could have been in circulation for up to seven years.[27] While the debate about the exact or most likely date of Mark's Gospel continues, we have to admit that even the forties of the first century is not an early, but a late dating. No one, so far, has produced a single convincing reason why the Christians should have waited for ten years or more before they set pen to paper, given the fact that their neighbours, the rival messianic eschatological movement of the Essenes, produced, copied and distributed scroll after scroll to proclaim their own messianic vision. It should be obvious enough that a new movement which proclaimed the fulfilment of these Jewish hopes and expectations had to write down what they knew and believed. An oral tradition was valuable, but on its own, it was inadequate. The incident at Beroea proves the point: those pious Jews listened to Paul and Silas, to the oral tradition as it were, but afterwards, they studied the scriptures to find out if it was true. The scriptures first of all meant the prophetic writings of the 'Old Testament'. But imagine for a moment that the Christians had no scrolls of their own to be placed and studied next to the scrolls of the common Jewish heritage, not even by AD 47, when Paul spoke at Beroea. Would those Jews have taken their claims seriously? The producing of scrolls was of the essence. Nicholas Orme's question is as relevant as the answers suggested by Zuntz, Robinson and others.[28]

Jews, 'God-fearers' – those unconverted philosemites who participated in synagogal life – and of course the first Jewish Christians all used the libraries of the synagogues, at least until the eighties of the first century. It was only then, after the loss of the Temple, and in an attempt to clarify who really belonged to mainstream Judaism, that the groups which appeared heretical from the orthodox point of view were excluded. The so-called Council of Jamnia (Yafneh), some ten years after the destruction of the Temple, took the decisive step.[29] It was a conference of the utmost importance for the survival of organized Judaism, with heated debates about the restructuring of the cult and the official canon of the Jewish Bible.[30] After the famous Yohanan ben Zakkai convened the Pharisees at Jamnia with the express permission of the Roman authorities, other rabbis like Eliezer ben Hyrcanos, Joshua ben Hananyah and Rabban Gamaliel II took over, and it was the last of these, the grandson of Paul's teacher (mentioned in the New Testament), who introduced an additional text into the 'Eighteen Benedictions'. It was the curse on the 'Nozrim' – the followers of Yeshua ha-Nozri, Jesus the Nazorean, and the 'Minim', more generally all those sectarians who followed divisive teachings: 'May apostates have no hope and the kingdom of impertinence be uprooted in our day. May the Nozrim and Minim disappear in the twinkling of an eye. May they be removed from the book of the living and not be inscribed among the just. Blessed be you, O Lord, you who casts down the proud.'[31]

By the eighties of the first century, some fifteen years after the deaths of Peter and Paul, twenty years after the death of James, the brother of the Lord and leader of the church in Jerusalem, Christians had begun to concentrate on non-Jewish target groups anyway. They did not deny their Jewish roots – it is important to note, against the politically correct propaganda of some circles today, that Christian anti-Semitism did not begin with the New Testament, a collection of Jewish writings about a Jew, after all. Recent studies have shown conclusively that the polemical tone of the internal Jewish debate about the true Messiah, as we find it occasionally in the pages of the New Testament (John 8.12–59; Mark 2.23—3.6; Matthew 12.22–42), was the style of the day, so to speak, and was mild in comparison with the tone of the diatribes that the Essenes at Qumran aimed at fellow-Jews in their writings.[32] The first recognizably anti-Semitic writings by Christian authors are Justin Martyr's *Dialogue with Trypho, c.* AD 155, and Melito of Sardis' *Easter Homily* of *c.* AD 160, which condemns the Jews as the murderers of God.[33] At that stage, Christianity had indeed lost, if not actually suppressed, its sense of Jewishness. But in New Testament times, the links were closer than the separations. And the first Christians owed their familiarity with libraries to their Jewish roots and connections.

The synagogal library at Beroea is a prime example in the Diaspora, but, apart from the Qumran library system, we have at least one striking case from Judaea: the library of the synagogue on Masada. It was discovered by Yigael Yadin, during his excavation of the fortress, between 1963 and 1965, and was in use until the occupation by the Romans in AD 73/4.[34] Although only a few fragmentary manuscripts have survived, hidden under the floor, it obviously was a mixed study and reference library. Deuteronomy was found there (a fragment of chapters 33—34, with the final blessing of Moses), Ezekiel (the surviving chapter was ch. 37, the one about hope in a bodily resurrection), Jesus ben Sirach (Ecclesiasticus) chs 39–44, apocryphal additions to Joshua, numerous *ostraca*, potsherds with Hebrew quotes and notices, and a text associated with the Essenes, 'Serekh Shiroth 'Olath ha-Shabbat', the Angelic Liturgy of the Sabbath Sacrifice.[35] Outside the synagogue, the Jews on Masada kept collections of other texts, among them letters and potsherds in Greek. Even the nationalists and Zealots who defended Masada against the Romans were trilingual, writing and reading Hebrew, Aramaic and Greek with ease.[36]

The debate about the exact nature of the Qumran library will continue for many years to come. Was it a collection of biblical scrolls and Essene writings only? Was it, as some still think, the library of the Temple of Jerusalem hidden in the caves just before the Roman onslaught on Jerusalem? Or was it a mixed collection with documents from several Jewish movements, collected by the Essenes and combined with their own writings? Even the fragmentary state of the finds (some scholars assume that only 6 per cent of the original holdings have been recovered) still betrays a well-thought-out system. Three sections can be distinguished: (1) biblical texts in Hebrew, as well as translations into Aramaic (Targumim) and Greek (the Septuagint); (2) apocrypha

113

and pseudepigraphical books – such as *Tobit*, *Enoch*, the *Book of Jubilees*, the *Testament of Levi*, and many others; (3) previously unknown new writings associated with the movement, including commentaries on biblical books (the Habakkuk Pesher and others) and the community's messianic, eschatological and disciplinary teaching – for example, the Manual of Discipline, the Damascus Document, the Temple Scroll, the Letter of the Teacher of Righteousness, the Thanksgiving Hymns, new psalms, the Copper Scroll, and others. These new writings have excited much speculation and some outlandish theories about Jesus, John the Baptist, Paul, James and the Essenes. No serious scholar believes in the plausibility of these fantasies. What concerns us here is the character of the library system as such.

The people who lived at Qumran had established their main library 'building' within sight of the settlement: it was the cave now called Cave 4, with up to 800 scrolls. Other, smaller cave libraries were partly in view, and partly spread all over the surrounding area, many of them out of sight. Three of them, Caves 6 to 8, could only be accessed through the main settlement. Small and largely destroyed, the mixed holdings of 6 and 8 do not offer any clues as to the reason why they were so close to the settlement. Cave 7, however, appears to have been a 'poison cabinet' of exclusively Greek writings only on papyrus – a unique phenomenon at Qumran – which many scholars have described as a collection of texts used and written by Jewish Christians. It seems the Qumran Essenes, who had heard about the new messianic movement, wanted to study their first writings, and as the jar with the Hebrew inscription 'Rome' implies, they got these scrolls from the large Jewish community in Rome (some 60,000 Jews lived in Rome at the time), probably just before AD 68, rather than causing suspicion by buying them in Jerusalem. If at least two of the Greek papyrus fragments found in Cave 7 really are Jewish Christian texts (Mark and 1 Timothy), then this unique cave, too, was arranged according to the 'three-tiered' library system: first, biblical scrolls (Exodus has been found: fragment 7Q1), second, apocrypha (a fragment of the *Letter of Jeremiah* = *Baruch* 6, 7Q2), and third, new, group-specific writings (Mark, 7Q5; 1 Timothy, 7Q4). From a Jewish Christian perspective, the combination of such writings would have made sense. The Torah, of which Exodus has survived in the cave, constituted the Law, without which Christian thinking and teaching was inconceivable. Texts like the *Letter of*

Jeremiah belonged to those popular writings which could be used to explain how Jewish thinking had developed towards the message proclaimed by Jesus. And the oldest Gospel, Mark's, was the historical document about this Jesus which would have explained to Jews and non-Jews alike who the Messiah was, and how ancient prophecies had been fulfilled in him and by him. A letter like 1 Timothy, finally, written in Rome from where the collection had come to Qumran, would have cast useful light on the community system of the Jewish Christians, their teaching on structure and authority, and could be compared, by the Essenes, to their own manuals. One of the leading Jewish Qumran scholars, Shemaryahu Talmon, was among those who suggested that the Essenes at Qumran were the most likely people to collect these rival writings straight away.[37]

It was in the best interests of these two messianic, eschatological movements, the Essenes and the Christians, to spread their thoughts as quickly and as widely as possible. Everyone, after all, should have a fair chance to learn and change their ways. The Essenes, it seems, restricted their missionary activities to Jewish communities throughout the Roman Empire. They were not interested in reaching the Gentile world.[38] But the Jewish Christians, as we have seen again and again, targeted Jews and non-Jews, as Jesus had done from the very beginning of his ministry. Their teaching was not confined to a closed community. Their texts were to be made available to a wider readership: both the old scripture – i.e. the Torah, the prophets, the psalms and the historical writings of their Jewish heritage – and the new. Every member of the community, not just the initiated elite, everyone who could hear or read, was included: 'Greet all the brothers and sisters with a holy kiss,' Paul writes in 1 Thessalonians 5.26–7; 'I solemnly command you by the Lord that this letter be read to all of them.' Writings are passed on and exchanged: 'And when this letter has been read among you, have it read also in the church of the Laodiceans. And see that you read also the letter from Laodicea' (Colossians 4.16). Even the book of Revelation insists on the importance of an accessible, written form of teaching and communicating: John is not told to visit the seven churches in Asia Minor and to have a nice chat with them, he is told to send them letters (Revelation 1.11). Reaching the Gentile world was another, more demanding step. They had to find outlets beyond their own circles. And as it happened, bookshops and lending libraries already existed in the Greek-speaking East and the Latin-speaking West.

Some publishers and booksellers of those times are known to us from extant sources. In Athens, for example, there was a lively market in books, both for new publications and for the classics. But it was very much a 'supply and demand' situation. Scrolls were copied by hand, and thus, technically speaking, every single scroll was a new edition. Professional copyists had to be employed, and some authors, like the philosopher Aristotle, distinguished between works they wanted to be published widely – in his case, those in refined prose – and those they wanted to be read only by their own students. The latter texts never reached a general public.[39] Cicero's friend Titus Pomponius Atticus (110–32 BC) was a successful entrepreneur, publisher and bookseller, first in Athens, then in Rome; he copied and distributed Cicero's works. Martial, the poet whom we met briefly in Chapter 6, had a favourite bookseller, and he praises him in one of his epigrams:

> If you want to take my books with you, wherever you go,
> So that they may accompany you on long journeys,
> Go and buy those small paperback editions;
> Others fill your bookshelves, but mine are handy.
> However, do not be ignorant and do not look in vain
> All over Rome. I'll tell you where to go and find them:
> Go straight to Secundus who once served under the learned
> Lucensis.
> You will find him behind the Temple of Pax, at the Palladian
> Market.[40]

Martial's pocket-sized editions were of the classics – of Virgil (with frontispiece), Ovid, Homer, and his own writings. Elsewhere, the best-selling scrolls were those of the epic writers and the dramatists, lyric poets, and, in the Hellenistic period, of story-telling prose writers. The great thinkers and philosophers, authors like Cicero and Seneca in the West, and Plato and Aristotle in the East, also had their niches. But scrolls, even the pocket books, remained expensive. Occasionally, private collectors borrowed a scroll and had it copied or copied it themselves. But in New Testament times, every major city – not just a metropolis like Alexandria – had a public library which was no longer reserved for the small cultural elite of philologists and other scholars. At long last, after centuries of restricted access, anyone who could read and was of good standing was allowed into these libraries with their representative cross-section of literature, poetry, history and philosophy – and 'philosophy', in those days, was a term which also covered what we would call 'theology'.[41] Julius Caesar had introduced the first public reading library in Rome, with a Greek and a Latin section, and the emperors either expanded it or built their own libraries.

For Christians, this was a welcome starting point. Their writings could be sold on the market, provided they found booksellers like Secundus. And a Gospel like Mark's, short enough for a handy scroll, would have been an interesting novelty, with its brilliant beginning which we discussed in Chapter 3, and its innovative, unheard-of combination of allusions to the cult of the emperor and an unknown hero who, like the emperor, was a son of God – and all of it in masterful Greek. At a time when Mark's book about Jesus was not yet called a 'Gospel' and when there was no New Testament, nor an organized Church, his text had to survive on its own merits, if it was to succeed outside the tighter circle of Jewish Christians and Gentile 'God-fearers'. And this dual approach of doing something absolutely revolutionary, writing about a Jew from Roman Palestine, in social terms a man of lowly and uncertain origins, but doing so with linguistic artistry of the highest order and within the framework of imperial terminology, may have opened another door: the one to the public libraries. Religious texts, the teaching of the cults and sects, was neither sold publicly nor available in the libraries. There were two ways around this. The first was to present it as philosophy, the 'love of wisdom', as the Greek-speaking Jews in Alexandria had apparently done successfully enough to get the Torah into the library of Alexandria, with the help of the great Demetrius. The Christians could hardly follow this example, since they had no first-generation writings of this nature. However, the four Gospels could be presented as historical biographies in the Hellenistic mould. For such a strategy, Mark's first sentence was a stroke of genius. Not many years later, in the mid- to late fifties, Luke went a step further. He not only dedicated his Gospel to a high-ranking Roman official, His Excellency (*kratistos*) Theophilus, he also introduced the work with a prologue which followed all the rules of the Greek historical school: describing the method of research, referring to the historian's process of selecting and structuring the material, and outlining the purpose of the enterprise:

> Since many have undertaken to set down an orderly account of the events that have been fulfilled among us, just as they were handed on to us by those who from the beginning were eyewitnesses and servants of the word, I too decided, after investigating everything carefully from the very first, to write an orderly account for you, Your Excellency Theophilus, so that you may know the truth concerning the things about which you have been instructed. (Luke 1.1–4)[42]

Both Mark's and Luke's Gospels were tailored to the market: they were Hellenistic biographies within an historian's framework, and, what may have mattered as well, they were written in excellent Hellenistic Greek. It should not surprise us if these two Gospels, perhaps more so than Matthew and John, reached the Gentile markets very soon, including the public libraries. Luke's dedication served a further purpose: it guaranteed access to Theophilus' circle of influence. And we know that the strategy worked: volume 2, the Book of Acts, is dedicated to the same Theophilus (Acts 1.1). If His Excellency had refused to accept the message, or if Luke had felt that Theophilus was hesitant, the second dedication would never have been made. But Acts is indeed dedicated to Theophilus.

We should not underestimate the effectiveness of this complex infrastructure of bookshops and libraries. It contributed to the early success of the Christian message. And yet, this was just one vehicle for spreading the good news of Jesus in a multicultural Graeco-Roman environment. Oral tradition remained as valuable as the literary tradition, at least as long as the eyewitnesses of the first generation were available (see Acts 1.21–6). And individual Christians or whole communities could always follow the example of the Greek orator Demosthenes (384–322 BC): he copied the work of the historian Thucydides no fewer than eight times, in his own hand, and it should be assumed that he did so because he wanted others to possess the great man's historical scrolls.[43] Individual copying, or dictating to a group of scribes, had been done before, as did the first Christians. During the first century, only the comparatively brief period of the Neronian persecution, from late AD 64 or early 65 until the death of Nero on 9 June 68, interrupted Christian publishing and copying of texts. There is no evidence of any attempt to interfere with these activities at any other time in the first century.[44]

The efficiency of the Christians' distribution system soon surpassed that of the Jews and the Romans; eventually, the first identifiable Christian public libraries were established, long before Christianity became a legally accepted religion under Licinius and Constantine and their Edict of Milan in AD 313. At least six Christian librarians can be identified by name: Alexander of Jerusalem, who established the library in Jerusalem in AD 212; his colleague Julius Africanus, who had helped Emperor Severus Alexander (222–35) set up the library of the Pantheon in Rome before he became a Christian philosopher and settled in Emmaus-Nicopolis; and three figures previously mentioned in this chapter – Pantaenus in Alexandria, with the library of the Christian academy, the Didascaleion; his pupil Origen, who founded the library of Caesarea Maritima in AD 231; his colleague and successor Pamphilus; and, not least, the church historian Eusebius (AD 265–340), bishop and director of the library at Caesarea.[45] An earlier Christian library existed under Bishop Polycarp of Smyrna; it must pre-date his death in AD 156. Smyrna, of course, was a model city in this respect: the public library was famous enough to be singled out by the geographer Strabo in the early first century AD.[46] Earlier still, Ignatius of Antioch, who was martyred *c.* AD 109, debated with opponents who had studied Gentile, Jewish and Jewish Christian scrolls in the Archeion, the library of Antioch.[47]

With the early third century and the period of Constantine, we have left New Testament times. However, it is important to keep in mind that these later developments were made possible by the cosmopolitan attitudes of the first Christians, and by their knowledge, experience and strategy. The first Christians knew what they were doing, and the community of John, who edited his Gospel, may have concluded the scroll with a knowing smile: 'But there are many other things that Jesus did; if every one of them were written down, I suppose that the world itself could not contain the books that would be written' (John 21.25). The Christian message was spread at a previously unknown speed and efficiency, among Jews, Greeks and Romans.[48] No later period surpassed these achievements of the century of Jesus.

7 Test Cases: An Epilogue

> Just as he was speaking, a cock crowed.
>
> Petronius, *Satyrica* 73.6

> So when they had come together, they asked him: 'Lord, is this the time when you will restore the kingdom of Israel?' He replied: 'It is not for you to know the times or periods that the Father has set by his own authority. But you will receive power when the Holy Spirit has come upon you; and you will be my witnesses in Jerusalem, in all Judaea and Samaria, and to the ends of the earth.'
>
> Acts 1.6–8

Taking note

The historical Jesus was a man who could write but who, like other great teachers of Judaism and Graeco-Roman antiquity, left the recording of his sayings and actions to his followers. Had he intended to write himself, his literary competence would have extended to Hebrew, Aramaic and Greek. The old scholarly myth of an illiterate carpenter who just about managed to speak Aramaic with a strong Galilean accent has been laid to rest. And like Socrates, who noticed that Plato was writing down what he said, like the rabbis who saw others taking notes of their utterances, Jesus surely was aware of individuals around him taking shorthand notes, scribbling easily memorized sayings on potsherds (*ostraca*), wax tablets, or scraps of papyrus. We do not know of any specific incidents of this, as none are mentioned in the Gospels, but one at least can be reconstructed hypothetically. Matthew's Gospel, which, from the earliest days of church historiography, was associated with the disciple Levi-Matthew, contains more speeches, and longer ones, than the other synoptic Gospels, but the longest of them all, the Sermon on the Mount, precedes the calling of Levi-Matthew into the inner circle of the twelve disciples. Assuming that those early commentators who identified the Gospel author with the tax collector were correct in their assumption, here, in the guise of an epilogue, is a real-life test case.

Levi-Matthew was a tax and customs official in charge of a frontier, collecting duty and taxes at the border between the tetrarchy of Philip and the Galilean territory of Herod Antipas, including the tax levied on fishing.[1] These collectors of tolls, customs and taxes, the *telōnai* in Greek, were despised by other Jews, because they were seen partly as collaborators with the vassal kings of the Romans, and partly as sinners who gained their wealth by exploiting their position (cf. Mark 2.13–17; Matthew 9.9–13; Luke 5.27–32, 15.1). But in order to be appointed, they had to speak Greek, the international language of trade and commerce, and they had to possess certain other professional skills. One of them was shorthand note-taking. Shorthand writing was known among Greek-speaking Jews at least since the days of the Septuagint. The second- to third-century BC Greek translation of Psalm 42.5 contains a reference to the shorthand writer, the *oxygraphos*. It should be obvious that such a technical term made sense only if the target group, Greek-speaking Jews, knew and understood it. The Hebrew text of Psalm 45.2 has the expression *sōfēr māchēr*, which means the skilled, fast writer. At the time of the Greek translation, abbreviated forms of writing, called 'brachygraphy' (from *brachys*, 'short'), tachygraphy (from *tachys*, 'swift', 'quick', 'short') and 'oxygraphy' (from *oxys*, 'quick', 'fast', 'sharp'), had come into use. It is unlikely that Jewish scribes of the third century BC invented any of them from scratch, but Psalm 45.2 shows us that they were among the first to use one. At that time, every scribe or group of scribes had their own, individual system. The first scribe who introduced a systematic shorthand notation was Tiro, the secretary of Cicero (106–43 BC); hence, they are called the 'Tironian notes'. In other words, shorthand writing was developed and used in Greek and Latin some time before the Roman emperors began to rule the Holy Land.[2] In the cosmopolitan world of Jesus, Levi-Matthew – like many educated Jews before and after him – was fully aware of such techniques and knew how to use them.

Jesus, the wandering preacher, went up on a mountainside 'when he saw the crowds' who 'followed him from Galilee, the Decapolis, Jerusalem, Judaea and the region across the Jordan' (Matthew 5.1, 4.25). The place was not far from Capernaum (Matthew 8.5). In the vicinity, Levi-Matthew had his customs and tax office – the harbour installations where the office would have been situated, 800 metres long, were identified by archaeologists several years ago.[3] The news that Jesus, the famous preacher, was walking up the mountain nearby, apparently ready to teach the masses, would have reached him soon enough. He took the afternoon off and followed him up the hill, where he then sat with the others in the semicircle of the natural theatre described above in Chapter 2. After a short while, he began to take shorthand notes. Jesus, centre stage, noticed the person in the audience who was taking these notes, and, at the end of the session, made his enquiries. A couple of days later, Levi-Matthew has reread his notes. He understands the uniqueness of the message. When Jesus passes by and says, 'Follow me!', he is ready, gets up and follows him (Matthew 9.9). Taking his shorthand notes of Jesus' Sermon on the Mount with him, he records further speeches. They form the nucleus of his own Gospel and explain what Papias, the Bishop of Hierapolis, meant when he stated *c*. AD 110 that Matthew wrote down the sayings of Jesus ('ta logia') in Aramaic, and that everyone translated them as best he could.[4] Matthew's edited notes may indeed have been passed on to other followers and writers, including Luke, who used what he needed for his own Gospel. Matthew himself, using the published version of Mark for a model, took his notes and incorporated them, at length, into his own Greek Gospel. Most of the speeches were in Aramaic, a few in Greek.[5] Matthew was competent in both languages. And the timing of Matthew's calling – after, not before the Sermon on the Mount – helps us to correct the widespread assumption that the 'Sermon on the Plain' (Luke 6.17–49) is the same event, somehow misplaced by a helpless Luke. For here, in the incident chosen by Luke, we clearly have a separate and later occasion: Matthew is already a disciple of Jesus (Luke 5.27–32).

Needless to say, this is a reconstruction which operates within a strictly historical framework, where Matthew is allowed to write his own Gospel and where the Sermon on the Mount really did take place. But it is a reconstruction, not a deconstruction, and if we cannot prove the circumstantial ingredients with mathematical precision, neither should we fall into the trap of naivety which imprisons all those who do not want to accept that Levi-Matthew, Jesus, and the Jews in the region of Capernaum were real people in a real world. A Matthew who took shorthand was part of a society which did exist. And his Aramaic notes as the source for his and other Gospel authors' edited accounts of Jesus' speeches are more realistic by far than the popular theories about an alleged source 'Q' (from the German *Quelle*, 'source') – a document which is supposed to contain the textual material that is closely similar in Matthew's and Luke's Gospels but does not appear in Mark, and which permeates modern Gospel research but which no one has ever seen.[6] It is quite sufficient to assume that Matthew was his own and Luke's additional source, apart from the model and material supplied by Mark.

It must also be noted that 'Mark', 'Matthew', 'Luke' and 'John' should be understood as individual authors, and not as pseudonymous writers fictitiously presented by unknown communities. The case is clear enough with Luke, a Gospel, as we saw in Chapter 6, dedicated to His Excellency (*kratistos*) Theophilus (Luke 1.3; cf. Acts 1.1). There are no pseudonymous, let alone anonymous dedications in antiquity. It is a moot point that neither Luke's name, nor that of any of the others, is mentioned in their Gospels. One has yet to find a work of literature or historiography from those times where the author is identified in the main text. Texts published as scrolls had the author's name on a leather strap, a so-called *sillybos* or *sittybos* attached to the handle, or written on the outside of the scroll itself.[7] Later, with the codices, the name was placed on the cover and, eventually, it 'travelled' from there to the line above the beginning of the actual text – this is where we find it in the oldest codices of the New Testament.[8] Variations existed; for example, the authors' names were sometimes repeated in an endnote addition to the text.[9] Nothing has changed: even today, publishers put their authors' names on the spine, the cover, and the title page, and not in the text. Even if we assume the unlikely case that the first published Gospel, as the first example of its genre, did not have much more than, say, 'Gospel', 'euangelion', on its *sittybos*, it would have become necessary to add the author's name on the second and all further Gospels' leather straps, and retrospectively on further copies of the first Gospel, to avoid confusion. To put it differently, and Luke's case being obvious enough, the other Gospel authors, too, were identified as individuals at a time when fiction would have been impossible.[10]

At the same time, the gospel message was considered more important than the personalities of the authors. Ignatius, Bishop of Antioch (who, as noted earlier, died *c.* AD 109), knew and quoted from

123

Matthew's and John's Gospels in his letters without identifying their authors by name. He may have known 'John', supposed by many contemporaries to have been the Gospel author and (or?) the presbyter (elder) of the three Johannine letters, who was apparently still alive by AD 100.[11] About a year later, Papias, who knew John the Presbyter, and who wrote a *History of the Interpretation of the Sayings of the Lord* which has survived only in a few fragments, explicitly comments on the nature of the Gospels – particularly, in his surviving fragments, on Mark, Matthew and John – and mentions the names.[12] These non-anonymous writings, with Mark and Luke as models of excellent Hellenistic Greek and a memorable prose style – characteristics still underestimated by most New Testament scholars – were not mere 'school handbooks' for 'private', i.e. internal, Jewish Christian and Gentile Christian missionary purposes. Even the oldest surviving papyrus manuscripts, some of them first-century or early second-century copies, were already written in a clear, careful uncial style reminiscent of secular documentary texts, good enough to be acceptable to a cultivated pagan readership.[13]

Fire and alabaster

Richard Bauckham reminded readers of the New Testament that 'the evidence of early Christian literature (not least the Gospels) is that the early Christian movement had a strong sense of itself as a worldwide movement'. And he added: 'For Jewish Christians who made up most of the early Christian readership, this must have come naturally, since the communities of the Jewish diaspora were used to understanding themselves in terms of their common membership of a people scattered across the world.'[14] The same applied to Gentile converts, particularly where and when they had been actively involved in their own literary culture, which was far from purely local. It is the rediscovery of this climate of writing, reading and communicating, which produced 'even' the first Christian historical, literary documents in the form of scrolls and codices written by individual authors with a story to tell, that has recently given rise to a new investigation. To conclude this book, let us look at one avenue in this investigation. It is a kind of appetizer, stimulating our curiosity, and it begins with a passage from Mark's Gospel:

While Peter was below in the courtyard, one of the servant-girls of the high priest came by. When she saw Peter warming himself, she stared at him and said, 'You also were with Jesus, the man from Nazareth.' But he denied it, saying, 'I do not know or understand what you are talking about.' And he went out into the forecourt. Then the cock crowed. And the servant-girl, on seeing him, began again to say to the bystanders, 'This man is one of them.' But again he denied it. Then after a little while the bystanders again said to Peter, 'Certainly you are one of them; for you are a Galilean.' But he began to curse, and he swore an oath, 'I do not know this man you are talking about.' At that moment the cock crowed for the second time. Then Peter remembered that Jesus had said to him, 'Before the cock crows twice, you will deny me three times.' And he broke down and wept.[15]

The cock was a very real animal in this story. Not far from the high priest's palace, the Roman garrison on the Antonia Fortress kept cocks. Their crow, for which there even exists a Greek technical term, *alektrophonia*, marked the night watch, and it may be assumed that the cockcrow after Peter's second denial announced the third watch from midnight to three o'clock in the morning.[16] In other words, no one present in the high priest's courtyard would have perceived it as being ominous, except Peter, of course, who was instantly reminded of Jesus' prophecy.

If Romans and others, whether Greek- or Latin-speaking, did think about the cock at all, it was in a benign, positive context: its presence was thought to guard against lions and demons in the desert; it could be understood as an erotic symbol (and it still is, of course, in colloquial English); and sacrificing it was meant to prevent illnesses.[17] Even the dying words of Socrates were about a cock: 'Crito, we owe Asclepius a cock. Sacrifice one to him, and do not forget it!'[18] But for the first time in Greek literature, Mark changes the cock's image. Here, in the scene in the courtyard, it is a symbol of something negative, of betrayal, even of perjury, preceding a catastrophic event, the death of Jesus. And this was such a remarkable alteration that its recurrence elsewhere in literature should attract our attention. Such a recurrence there is, in a work written about twenty years after Mark's Gospel: The *Satyrica* of Petronius.

Petronius was proconsul of Bithynia (one of the regions to which Peter's first letter was sent), became Emperor Nero's adviser on matters of taste, and was forced by Nero to commit suicide, after court intrigues, in AD 66. He is also one of the 'heroes' in Henryk Scienkiewicz's novel *Quo Vadis?*, the famous film of which started the career of Sir Peter Ustinov, who played Nero. But in real life, Petronius also was the author of the first Roman satirical novel, finished just before his death. Only fragments have survived, and one of them is the central story, the so-called 'Cena Trimalchionis', the 'Banquet of Trimalchio'. This Trimalchio is a wealthy parvenu, of vulgar tastes, and Petronius portrays him as the typical *nouveau riche* who has risen from the lower classes. In the middle of a particularly decadent meal, we are told, Trimalchio suddenly declares:

> 'Friends, a slave of mine is celebrating his first shave today. He is a very orderly and meticulous man. So let's drink deep and serve up until dawn.' Just as he was speaking, a cock crowed. The sound disconcerted him to such an extent that he ordered wine to be poured under the table, and that the lamp be sprinkled with unmixed wine. And he even switched a ring to his right finger. 'It is no coincidence', he said, 'that this cock is giving us a sign. This either means that there will be a fire, or someone in the neighbourhood is about to die. Spare us! Whoever brings us this informer will be rewarded!'[19]

This is a remarkable scene. Against all expectations, and for the first time after Mark's Gospel, the cock is the harbinger of bad news. Trimalchio is frightened and in his panic, he resorts to numerous superstitious gestures. He interprets the cockcrow as quite catastrophic; he even fears impending death in the neighbourhood.

Petronius uses an interesting Latin word to describe the cock: *index*. It means informer, accuser, or even traitor. In this sense, it was used before Petronius, and it later occurs in a Christian context. In one of his letters to Emperor Trajan, Pliny the Younger (AD 62–113), who, like Petronius before him, served in the province of Bithynia, asks how he should deal with Christians who have been accused by anonymous informers. And the Latin word he uses for those informers is *index*.[20] In a nutshell, the Trimalchio of Petronius sees the cock not, as in all previous Latin literature, as a messenger of good tidings or as a protector, but as the animal which brings shattering news. It is a starting point. If one sees this as an echo of Mark, the only literary model Petronius could have used, one notices numerous other, even more direct allusions. Petronius seems to parody Mark's Gospel. Mark describes the anointing of Jesus in Bethany with ointment of nard from an alabaster jar. It happens at table, and everyone present is expected – just as much as we, today's readers of Mark, are expected – to understand it as presaging the death of Jesus (Mark 14.3–9). In the 'Banquet of Trimalchio', a decisive scene begins with Trimalchio, who says:

> 'I want to be carried out dead in glory, so that all the people will shout their blessings after me.' He promptly opened a flask of nard oil and anointed us all: 'I hope this will do me good in death as it does good for me in life!' He then had wine poured into a bowl: 'Now imagine you are invited here for my funeral banquet.' The whole thing made them feel like throwing up, when Trimalchio, now utterly drunk, ordered some trumpeters into the dining room for a strange recital. Propped up on a pile of cushions, he stretched out along the edge of the couch and said: 'Pretend I am dead, and play something beautiful.' The trumpets bawled out a funeral march.[21]

Once more, there is no parallel in classical literature for such a scene of an anointing with nard oil foreboding death, unless one sees this act as a bawdy parody of Mark's Gospel, with Trimalchio, the egomaniac, performing the anointing himself. In antiquity, nard or spikenard was an item of luxury, used also in erotic contexts. But never before Mark, and Petronius, who followed him, was it used in a scene of impending death, and as a symbol of death itself. At the same time, Petronius also parodies the Eucharist – see the previous quote from *Satyrica* 73.6–74.2 (on p. 126), and Mark 14.23–4. He does so again in another part of the *Satyrica*, the fragmentary chapter 141. Here, a certain Eumolpus announces: 'All those who are named in my will, except my own freedmen, will get what I have left them on this condition: if they cut my body into pieces and eat it in front of all the people.' Some commentators of this scene have thought that it refers to the Orphic or Bacchantic mysteries, and Eumolpus himself alludes to strange practices of meneating families. But although such cults did indeed exist, there was never before anyone who told people to eat his body.

Seen from the perspective of literary history, not of theology, this new concept was introduced into world literature by the first of the Gospels, Mark's: 'While they were eating, he took a loaf of bread, and after blessing it, he broke it, gave it to them, and said: "Take, this is my body"' (Mark 14.22). And the first author in Graeco-Roman antiquity to use – and parody – this scene was Petronius. In short, these and other examples from Petronius' *Satyrica* alert us to a neglected aspect of the spreading of the Gospel.[22] Later pagan authors continued in this vein. Chariton of Aphrodisias, for example, the author of the Hellenistic novel *Chaireas and Callirhoe*, used and parodied the Gospel account of the crucifixion and of the empty tomb.[23] Mark's Gospel is aimed at a wider readership, including educated Greeks and Romans, and we may assume that the first scrolls which reached cities like Athens, Antioch, Alexandria and of course Rome itself, where it was written, were offered to curious browsers at the bookstalls of markets like the one named after Pallas Athene in Rome, and that widely read bibliophiles like Petronius picked them up – not to be convinced by the message, but to be inspired by the latest trends, in Greek or Latin. In fact, if Petronius could read and use Mark's Gospel for his parodic purposes, it is obvious enough that his own readership was aware of this new book about a certain Jesus who claimed to be a rival of the emperor's, a 'son of God'. After all, a parody only works if the readers recognize the allusions.

In about AD 66, when the 'Banquet of Trimalchio' was published, its first target audience, Nero's court in Rome – much as that of Claudius before him – were well aware of the newfangled Christian message: among the circumstantial evidence for this we may count Paul and his letter to the Philippians (4.22). Were the first Christians irritated by the mocking use of their sacred stories? On one level, they certainly were. But on another level, they saw the opportunities. As long as the educated Graeco-Roman population in the Roman Empire read the Gospels in the first place, there was hope – in fact, as we know from later events, there was certainty – that parody would give place to inquisitiveness, and in the end, to a growing acceptance of the good news of Jesus. Christianity flourished in this cosmopolitan world because it attracted all layers of society with a unique message. And against a background of manifold influences, parallels and cross-fertilizations, the way the story of Jesus was told, by the eyewitnesses and the people who wrote it down, copied and distributed it, is as unique in world history as Jesus, the Christ, himself.

Notes

1 The Desert Lives: An Introduction

1 Biblioteca Medicea Laurenziana, Florence, PSI 2.124, with Matthew 10.17–23, 25–32 and Luke 22.40–50, 52–6, 61, 63–4. It was given the number '0171' in the lists of New Testament manuscripts.

2 Nestle–Aland, *Novum Testamentum Graece*, 27th edn (Stuttgart: 1993), pp. 684–718.

3 Acts 5.3–21, in Staatliche Museen, Berlin, P. 11765.

4 R. Kasser, *Papyrus Bodmer XVII* (Cologne and Geneva: 1961).

5 C. P. Thiede, 'Papyrus Bodmer L. Das neutestamentliche Papyrusfragment P73 = Mt 25,43/26,2–3', *Museum Helveticum*, 47 (1990), pp. 35–40.

6 The most detailed study of relevant stellar movements, Babylonian cuneiform tablets (some of them at the British Museum in London) and other surviving documents was published by the Austrian astronomer Professor Konradin Ferrari d'Occhieppo, *Der Stern von Bethlehem in astronomischer Sicht*, 4th edn (Giessen and Basel: 2003).

7 Suetonius, 'De Vita Caesarum', *Divus Augustus* 23.2.

8 *Complete Works of Oscar Wilde*, with an Introduction by Vyvyan Holland (Collins, London and Glasgow: 1966), pp. 929–30.

2 An Evening at the Theatre: At Home with Jesus

1 See J. Cook, 'Is This Where Jesus Bathed?', *Guardian*, 22 October 2003.

2 Cf., for example, S. J. Case, 'Jesus and Sepphoris', *Journal of Biblical Literature*, 45 (1926), pp. 14–22; B. Schwank, 'Das Theater von Sepphoris und die Jugendjahre Jesu', *Erbe und Auftrag*, 52 (1976), pp. 199–206; R. A. Batey, 'Is Not This the Carpenter?', *New Testament Studies*, 30 (1984), pp. 249–58, 'Jesus and the Theatre', *New Testament Studies*, 30 (1984), pp. 563–74, and *Jesus and the*

Forgotten City: New Light on Sepphoris and the Urban World of Jesus (Pasadena, Calif.: 2000).

3 Another reference to Jesus and his interest in building matters, not to be found in any other contemporary source, is the eighteen men who died when the tower of Siloam fell on them (Luke 13.4).

4 Josephus, *Life* 230; *Jewish War* 3.289–306.

5 See G. Kroll, *Auf den Spuren Jesu*, 11th edn (Leipzig: 1990), pp. 82–3, with plate and transcription.

6 For Mary's Davidic ancestry, see e.g. Romans 1.3 and Luke 1.32, passages which refer to Mary herself and not to the adoption of Jesus by Joseph which made him a descendant of David by law. For Joseph's Davidic lineage, see Matthew 1.16–17 etc.

7 Cf. Jerusalem Talmud, Yebamoth 8 (9b).

8 The documents of the Babata Archive have been published in several incomplete editions; the most recent and almost complete edition is N. Lewis (ed.), *Judean Desert Studies: The Documents from the Bar Kohba Period in the Cave of Letters* (Jerusalem: 1989). See also Y. Yadin, *The Finds from the Bar-Kokhba Period in the Cave of Letters* (Jerusalem: 1963).

9 See, above all, K. Rosen, 'Jesu Geburtsdatum, der Census des Quirinus und eine juedische Steuererklaerung aus dem Jahre 127 nC.', *Jahrbuch fuer Antike und Christentum*, 38 (1995), pp. 5–15; C. P. Thiede, *The Dead Sea Scrolls and the Jewish Origins of Christianity* (Oxford: 2000), pp. 85–8.

10 In Mark 1.10 and parallels (Matthew 3.16; Luke 3.22; John 1.32), God's Spirit descends on Jesus 'like a dove'. In later Christian art, the dove became the most popular image of the peace of God, and of the Holy Spirit.

11 In particular, the stories about Mary's parents, Joachim and Anna, Mary's own miraculous birth, details of the journey to Bethlehem, the birth of Jesus in a cave, the explanation that Jesus' brothers and sisters were merely half-brothers and -sisters from a previous marriage of (the subsequently widowed) Joseph, Mary's perpetual virginity, etc. The 'Protogospel' was written in praise of Mary and contains the seeds of most of the mariological teachings and doctrines of the Roman Catholic Church, although it was condemned in the West, under the influence of Jerome in the fifth century, who taught that Jesus' brothers and sisters were his cousins. For the text,

see E. Hennecke (ed.), *New Testament Apocrypha*, vol. 1 (London: 1973), pp. 374–88.

12 *Infancy Story of Thomas* 14.1–3, in Hennecke (ed.), *New Testament Apocrypha*, vol. 1, p. 397.

13 Cf. the analysis of one of the excavators who corroborates the date, against some others who prefer a later one: J. F. Strange, 'Sepphoris', *Anchor Bible Dictionary*, vol. 5 (New York: 1992), pp. 1090–3. See also Batey, *Jesus and the Forgotten City*.

14 *Letter of Aristeas*, 284–5.

15 Josephus, *Jewish Antiquities* 19.344–51, and the shorter account by Luke in Acts 12.19–23.

16 They remain to be discovered. The famous theatre at Bet Shean (Scythopolis), one of the major tourist attractions south of the Sea of Galilee, was built as late as the fourth century AD.

17 Aeschylus, *Agamemnon* 1624. Aeschylus uses a similar version in his *Prometheus*, 325; Euripides copied it in his *Bacchae*, 795, and between Aeschylus and Euripides, the lyric poet Pindar (518–445 BC) has a closely related variant in his *Pythian Ode* 2.94–5. The scene in Acts 25.23—26.32 displays Paul's virtuosity. Paul remarks that Jesus spoke Aramaic (26.14), but he of course re-translates it into Greek for the Roman procurator Festus, who – unlike King Agrippa and Queen Bernice – would not have understood Aramaic. At the end, Festus acknowledges Paul's vast knowledge: 'You are out of your mind, Paul! Too much learning is driving you insane!' (26.24).

18 *Aiolos* is a lost play of which only fragments have survived. Paul's quotation is in fragment 1024 Nauck; the line can also be found in a fragment from Menander's lost play *Thaïs*: fragment 187 Koerte/218 Kock. See A. Nauck, *Tragicorum Graecorum Fragmenta*, 2nd edn (Leipzig: 1889; repr. with addenda by B. Snell, Hildesheim: 1964).

19 See P. W. van der Horst, *The Sentences of Pseudo-Phocylides* (Leiden: 1978), p. 76; L. B. Bernard (ed.), *St. Justin Martyr. The Second and First Apologies* (New York and Mahwah, NJ: 1997), 37.128, 146. The collection of treatises on the Unity of God is traditionally known under the title *De Monarchia*.

20 Josephus knew him and was introduced by him to Nero's wife Poppaea: *Life* 16.

21 The first outspoken criticism was late, however: Tertullian dedicated a whole treatise to the subject, *De Spectaculis*, written *c.* AD 198 (see also his *Apologeticum* 15.1–3 and *Against the Valentinians* 14). Tertullian may have been expressing more trenchantly a sentiment which had been felt before – see Theophilus of Antioch (*c.* AD 120–190), *To Autolychus* 3.15.

22 Novatian, *De Spectaculis* 3.2, *c.* AD 250.

23 Tacitus, *Germania* 19. Tacitus was not the first Roman author to complain about the theatre or to mock it; cf. also Pliny the Elder (AD 23–79), *Natural History* 7.184; Martial (AD 40–102), *Epigrams* 5.78, 26. See also Pliny the Younger (AD 62–114), *Letters* 7.14, 4–7.

24 Josephus, *Jewish Antiquities* 19.94. Cf. Martial, *De Spectaculis* (*Epigrammaton*) 7.4; Juvenal, *Satura* 8.187–8; Suetonius, *Caligula* 57.

25 Josephus, *Jewish Antiquities* 18.63–4.

26 The first of these was Alexander Polyhistor (105–38 BC), *On the Jews*. Alexander lived in Miletus and Rome. Nothing has survived complete; for the fragments see C. Mueller (ed.), *Fragmenta Historicum Graecorum*, (Paris: 1841–70), pp. 206–44. Practically all these fragments have survived thanks to quotes in the writings of Josephus, Clement of Alexandria and Eusebius of Caesarea. Alexander's *On the Jews* is quoted extensively in Eusebius' *Praeparatio Evangelica* 9.17–39, a passage which comments on Ezekiel and quotes numerous further fragments from his play. (The shorter reference by Clement of Alexandria is in his *Stromateis* 1.23.) For an English text of the passage on Ezekiel and his *Exagōgē*, see also M. Stern (ed.), *Greek and Latin Authors on Jews and Judaism*, vol. 1 (Jerusalem: 1976), pp. 161–2. For editions of all surviving fragments of the *Exagōgē*, see B. Snell and R. Kannicht (eds), *Tragicorum Graecorum Fragmenta*, 2nd edn (Goettingen: 1986), no. 128; English translation in H. Jacobsen, *The Exagoge of Ezechiel* (London: 1983).

27 Ezekiel must have written more than one drama. Clement of Alexandria called him 'the Poet of Jewish Tragedies' (*Stromateis* 1.23), Eusebius knew him as 'the Poet of Tragedies' (*Praeparatio Evangelica* 9.28.1). A damaged papyrus discovered in the Wadi Murabba'at, near the Dead Sea, P. Mur. 108, has been tentatively identified as fragments from an unknown play by Ezekiel, provisionally called *Iōsēph en Aigyptō* (Joseph in Egypt). See Thiede, *The*

Dead Sea Scrolls and the Jewish Origins of Christianity, pp. 77–80 (Greek edition with reconstruction forthcoming).

28 For circumstantial evidence in favour of the performance of Ezekiel's plays in public, see B. Snell, 'Ezechiels Moses-Drama', *Antike und Abendland*, 13 (1967), pp. 150–64; E. Starobinski-Safran, 'Un poète judéo-hellénistique: Ezéchiel le tragique', *Museum Helveticum*, 31 (1974), pp. 216–24; G. W. E. Nickelsburg, 'The Bible Rewritten and Expanded', in M. Stone (ed.), *Jewish Writings of the Second Temple Period* (Assen and Philadelphia: 1984), pp. 125–30.

29 The dramatic structure of Mark's Gospel has been recognized before. See, among others, G. Bilezikian, *The Liberated Gospel: A Comparison of the Gospel of Mark and Greek Tragedy* (Grand Rapids: 1977); B. Standaert, *L'Évangile selon Marc: Composition et genre littéraire* (Bruges: 1978); F. J. Matera, *What Are They Saying About Mark?* (New York and Mahwah, NJ: 1987), pp. 75–85.

30 Tertullian, *De Spectaculis* 29–30.

31 Latin text, introduction and commentary in (among others) K. Langosch, *Geistliche Spiele* (Darmstadt: 1961), pp. 99–105.

32 Cf. B. C. Crisler, 'The Acoustics and Crowd Capacity of Natural Theatres in Palestine', *Biblical Archaeologist*, 39 (1976), p. 137.

3 Who is Who? Emperors, Miracle Workers and Sons of God

1 Philo of Alexandria, *Legatio ad Gaium* 154.

2 Suetonius, *Vespasian* 23.4.

3 P. Oxy. 1453, 11, dated to 30/29 BC. Even Julius Caesar, whose status as *divus* (the divine one) had been established by a *consecratio* after his death on the instigation of his adoptive son Octavianus, the later Augustus – a move which made Augustus a *filius divi*, a son of the divine one, or in Greek, a *huios theou*, a son of God – had been styled a god by the grateful citizens of the Thessalian city Demetrias after a victorious battle: 'Gaius Iulius Caesar, autocrat, God' (H. W. Pleket and R. S. Stroud (eds), *Supplementum epigraphicum Graecum*, XIV (Amsterdam), p. 474).

4 For example, Acts 2.9, 6.9, 16.6, 19.1, 10, 22–7, 20.4, 16–18, 27.2; Romans 16.5; 1 Corinthians 16.19; 2 Corinthians 1.8; 2 Timothy 1.15; 1 Peter 1.1; Revelation 1.4.

5 Psalm 82.6–8 reads: 'I had thought: "Are you gods, are you all sons of the Most High? No! you will die as human beings do. As one man, princes, you will fall." Arise, God, judge the world, for all nations belong to you.' (Translation mine; cf. Thiede, *The Dead Sea Scrolls and the Jewish Origins of Christianity*, pp. 192–204.) See also Ezekiel 28.1–10.

6 Suetonius, *Vespasian* 7.1–3, and see below, note 14.

7 Cf. E. L. Bowie, 'Apollonius of Tyana', *Aufstieg und Niedergang der roemischen Welt* II.16.2 (1978), pp. 1652–99; E. Koskenniemi, *Apollonius von Tyana in der neutestamentlichen Exegese* (Tuebingen: 1994).

8 Philostratus, *Vita Apollonii* IV.10.

9 Philostratus, *Vita Apollonii* IV.45.

10 Philostratus, *Vita Apollonii* VIII.6–7. Cf. D. S. du Toit, *Theios Anthropos* (Tuebingen: 1997), p. 293.

11 We should agree with a growing scholarly consensus, particularly among classical philologists and historians, that the Gospels are not late and second-hand community creations. They were written during the four decades after the death of Jesus and published before the watershed year of AD 70, when Jerusalem and the Temple were destroyed. John A. T. Robinson broke the mould when he suggested such a re-dating (*Redating the New Testament*, London: 1976), and in spite of numerous attempts, his arguments have never been refuted. See, more recently, summaries of the debate in C. P. Thiede and M. d'Ancona, *The Jesus-Papyrus* (London: 1996), and U. Victor, 'Einleitung', in U. Victor, C. P. Thiede and U. Stingelin (eds), *Antike Kultur und Neues Testament* (Basel: 2003), pp. 13–29; all with further references.

12 See M. Sordi, *The Christians and the Roman Empire*, 2nd edn (London and New York: 1988, 1994), pp. 38–43 on Vespasian and Christianity.

13 Tacitus, *Historia* 4.81.1–3; Suetonius, *Vespasian* 7.2–3; Cassius Dio, *Roman History* 65.8.1–2.

14 For spittle as a recipe against eye diseases, see the miracle performed by Jesus in John 9.1–12, and Pliny the Elder, *Natural History* 28.37, 67. Pliny wrote his unfinished *Natural History* between AD 77 and his death in AD 79, i.e. after the spreading of the written and oral Gospel message. For treading on hands, cf. B.

Kollmann, *Jesus und die Christen als Wundertaeter* (Goettingen: 1996), particularly n. 122, with sources and references.

15 Talmud, b Brakhot 33a. The best-known apologist for Hanina ben Dosa has been Geza Vermes, e.g. 'Hanina ben Dosa', *Journal of Jewish Studies*, 23 (1972), pp. 28–50; 24 (1973), pp. 51–64.

16 Acts 28.3–6 has the story of Paul and the viper on Malta. While he was gathering brushwood, a snake 'fastened itself on his hand'. The natives first thought that Paul would die, but when, after a long while, they saw that nothing unusual had happened to him, 'they changed their minds and began to say he was a god'. Here, as in Hanina's story, the snake bites, but without any demonstrative provocation by Paul, who then merely throws it into the fire where it dies a 'natural' death, quite unrelated to any poisonous power of the victim's blood.

17 Brakhot 34b; cf. Luke 7.1–10 etc.

18 The exact dates of the rabbinic sources are disputed, but there is no manuscript evidence prior to the early Middle Ages.

19 Talmud, Taanit 23a.

20 Midrash Bereshit Rabba 13.7.

21 Taanit 23a.

22 As the classical philologist Ulrich Victor puts it: 'The historian has no choice but to accept the miracle healings of Jesus in the New Testament as factual events which, in whatever way, were outside everyday human experience. Today's philologists and historians, provided they are not prepared to abandon the field to the theologians from the outset, take the synoptic gospels and the Acts of the Apostles, in contrast with most theologians, not only for sources like other sources of antiquity, but for particularly reliable ones': U. Victor, 'Die Religionen und religioesen Vorstellungen im roemischen Reich', in U. Victor *et al.* (eds), *Antike Kultur und Neues Testament*, p. 115. Cf. A. D. Nock, 'Early Gentile Christianity and its Hellenistic Background', in A. D. Nock, *Essays on Religion and the Ancient World* (Oxford: 1972), vol. 1, pp. 49–133; A. N. Sherwin-White, *Roman Society and Roman Law in the New Testament* (Oxford: 1963), pp. 186–93.

23 The origin of this incongruous conclusion is the mistaken belief in the existence of 'good' manuscripts. There is no such thing. A correct reading may be contained in a very old or a much more

recent papyrus; it may be found in many manuscripts or in just one. Scribal errors and variants crept into the textual tradition of the New Testament, as into all other writings from antiquity, at a very early stage. The proper method is the careful eclectic analysis of these readings, one by one, doing justice to internal criteria of philology and exegesis, and, if necessary, to external criteria of scribal habits, the dates of manuscripts and the relations between them, and the details of geography, archaeology, and so forth. Textual criticism is not a mechanical exercise. As the leading classical scholar and Homer expert Martin L. West put it: 'That is what textual criticism is about: rightness! Which does not mean treating the external evidence in a cavalier fashion, but treating it critically, not giving systematic preference to some particular source or type of source. This brings us back to the axiom . . . that the editor should be a thinking being, not a puller of levers' (concluding remark of his 'Response by West on Nagy and Nardelli on West', *Bryn Mawr Classical Review*, 9 June 2001). Readers interested in finding out how New Testament editors still prefer to pull levers will find ample evidence in the analysis of the Gadara/ Gerasa episode in B. M. Metzger (ed.), *A Textual Commentary on the Greek New Testament*, 2nd edn (Stuttgart: 1994), pp. 18–19, 72, 121.

24 Cf., for contemporary eyewitness evidence, the autobiography of Josephus, *Life* 42.

25 For details about the excavation, the coins and their interpretation, see M. Nun, *Der See Genezareth und die Evangelien* (Giessen: 2001), pp. 70–2, 194–204.

26 Origen, *Commentary on John* 6.41, written as late as *c.* AD 248.

27 The New Testament leaves of the codex and most of the surviving Old Testament ones are on display at the British Library; 43 Old Testament leaves are at Leipzig University Library, where Constantin von Tischendorf deposited them in 1844; 12 leaves are at St Catherine's Monastery, Sinai, where the whole codex had been housed. The Codex Vaticanus, in the Vatican Library, may be as old as the Sinaiticus; some scholars think it is earlier, others suggest it is slightly later.

28 For example, the otherwise informative and innovative study by B. Pixner, *Wege des Messias und Staetten der Urkirche*, 3rd edn

(Giessen: 1996), pp. 142–8, with further references. See also Z. Safrai, 'Gerasa or Gadara?', *Jerusalem Perspective*, 51 (1996), pp. 16–19.

29 Even later there is a somewhat imprecise tradition in the Talmud (Shebi'it 6.1/36c) which may be understood as a reference to Gergesites living in the Decapolis near Hippos (Susitha).

30 Caesarea Maritima and Alexandria have been suggested as alternative places of origin, but the overwhelming evidence points to Rome. For an exhaustive survey of the arguments, see, above all, R. H. Gundry, *Mark: A Commentary on his Apology for the Cross* (Grand Rapids: 1993), pp. 1026–45.

31 Anaximander, *On Nature*, frags Diels I.15, 24, etc., in H. Diels and W. Krautz (eds), *Vorsokratiker I*, 9th edn (Berlin: 1959), pp. 81–90.

32 Plato, *Phaedrus* 245d–246a.

33 Aristotle, *Poetics* 7.1–7. On the text and its distribution see the edition by D. W. Lucas, *Aristotle: Poetics* (Oxford: 1968; repr., with corrections, 1972).

34 Homer, *Odyssey* 14.152, 166.

35 Cicero, *Letters to Atticus* 2.3, 1 and 13.39, 1.

36 For a detailed analysis, see C. P. Thiede and M. d'Ancona, *The Quest for the True Cross* (London: 2000), pp. 59–107.

37 Philo of Alexandria, *On Sobriety*, 56.

4 Crossing Borders: Jesus in Galilee and Syrophoenicia, and at the Shrine of Pan

1 For further details on the dating of the Gospels, see Chapter 6.

2 In some circles, Luke is thought to have been a Gentile who may have become a 'God-fearer', near to Judaism without converting, before he accepted Jesus and joined Paul's circle. This is based on a late and erroneous interpretation of Colossians 4.7–14, where Luke is allegedly singled out as a non-Jew. The Greek name Loukās, probably derived from Loukios, Lucius or Lucanus, may be of Latin origin, but of course there were Jews with 'non-Jewish' names in the Gospels – among them the two sons of Simon of Cyrene mentioned in Mark 15.21, Rufus (Latin) and Alexander (Greek), or the disciples from Bethsaida, Andrew (Simon Peter's brother) and Philip, or Stephen (Acts 6.5—7.60). The notion of Luke as a Gentile was

popularized as late as the early fifth century by Jerome (*Questiones hebraicae in Genesim*). Given the increasingly anti-Jewish stance of eastern Christianity from the mid-second century, one may assume that the misinterpretation of Colossians 4.14 was seen as a chance to find at least one New Testament author who was not a Jew. See also E. E. Ellis, *The Gospel of Luke* (London: 1966), pp. 52–3.

3 Seneca, *De superstitione* frag. 42, quoted in Augustine, *De civitate Dei* 6.11. On Seneca's contempt for the Jews, which makes this positive statement all the more remarkable, see, among others, P. Schaefer, *Judeophobia: Attitudes towards Jews in the Ancient World* (Cambridge, Mass. and London: 1997), pp. 111–13.

4 Cf. Y. Yadin, 'Masada', in M. Avi-Yonah and E. Stern (eds), *Encyclopaedia of Archaeological Excavations in the Holy Land*, vol. 3, (Jerusalem: 1997), p. 795 (on the schoolroom built by the rebels) and p. 809. Recent studies on the history of Masada have cast reasonable doubt on many aspects of the story told by Josephus in his *Jewish War* (7.252 ff.), but the continuous use of the synagogue and its library, including an extension during the revolt, remains well established. See also L. I. Levine, 'The Second Temple Synagogue: The Formative Years', in L. I. Levine (ed.), *The Synagogue in Late Antiquity* (Philadelphia: 1987), pp. 7–31.

5 See M. Nun, *Ancient Anchorages and Harbours around the Sea of Galilee* (Kibbutz En Gev: 1988), pp. 18–20; cf. also, on taxes for fishing, W. H. Wuellner, *The Meaning of 'Fishers of Men'* (Westminster: 1967), pp. 23–4, 43–4.

6 The oldest known reference which mentions the Via Maris and links it with the 'land beyond the Jordan' and south-western regions dates to the seventh century BC: Isaiah 9.1.

7 The famous 'Jesus Boat' discovered near Kibbutz Ginosar in January 1986, built in the late first century BC/early first century AD, shows the accuracy of a detail in Mark's Gospel: this type of boat, which could be rowed or sailed, had a platform at the stern for the helmsman, and a sheltered space under it. Here, a person could rest: 'But he [Jesus] was in the stern, asleep on a cushion' (Mark 4.38). Cf. S. Wachsmann, *The Excavations of an Ancient Boat in the Sea of Galilee (Lake Kinnereth)* (Jerusalem: 1990), p. 111.

8 Cf., for example, the Babylonian Talmud, Megilla 3.5 (224).

9 *Hellēnis* in Greek. Many modern translations obscure this inform-

ation; the NRSV, for example, falsifies the Greek text by offering 'a Gentile'. The NIV is more precise: 'a Greek'.

10 Juvenal, *Saturae* 3.12–14; Juvenal uses the Latin spelling of the word.

11 Juvenal, *Saturae* 6.542–3.

12 Pliny the Elder, *Natural History* 5.21; Josephus, *Jewish Antiquities* 18.107–28, and his description of the Battle of Bethsaida, against the Romans, in his *Life* 398–407.

13 Josephus, *Jewish Antiquities* 18.108.

14 For the evidence from coins, see F. Strickert, 'The Coins of Philip', in R. Arav and R. A. Freund (eds), *Bethsaida: A City by the North Shore of the Sea of Galilee* (Kirksville: 1995), pp. 165–89.

15 B. Pixner, 'Putting Bethsaida-Julias on the Map', *Christian News from Israel*, 27 (1982), pp. 165–70.

16 See J. Wilkinson, *Jerusalem Pilgrims before the Crusades* (Westminster: 1977), p. 128.

17 For a photo and reconstruction, see F. Strickert, *Bethsaida: Home of the Apostles* (Collegeville, Minn.: 1998), pp. 149–53; cf. Thiede and d'Ancona, *The Quest for the True Cross*, pp. 145–8, and B. Pixner, *Wege des Messias und Staetten der Urkirche*, 3rd edn (Giessen: 1996), pp. 127–41.

18 Josephus, *Jewish Antiquities* 17.21. His mother was Herod's fifth wife, Cleopatra of Jerusalem; the brothers Archelaus and Antipas (called 'the fox' by Jesus, Luke 13.32) were the sons of Malthace, a Samaritan.

19 Josephus, *Jewish Antiquities* 17.319; *Jewish War* 2.95.

20 Josephus, *Jewish Antiquities* 18.137 (where the dancer's name is mentioned), with Mark 6.17–22.

21 Josephus, *Jewish Antiquities* 18.4–10, 18.23–5; *Jewish War* 2.118, 2.433. Mark (3.18) and Matthew (10.4) call Simon the 'Cananaean', but this refers back to the Hebrew *qannâ'i* and Aramaic *qan'anâ*, which is the equivalent of the Greek *zēlōtēs*, zealot, denoting adherents of a religious party which saw its roots in the Maccabean revolt (see 1 Maccabees 2.27).

22 Josephus, *Jewish War* 4.1–54, 4.62–83.

23 Josephus, *Jewish War* 7.304–6.

24 The servant was the high priest's representative (cf. 2 Samuel 10.3–5; 1 Samuel 25.40–1); cutting off his ear rendered the high

priest himself unfit for public office. In other words, Peter's action was meant to end the Sadducean rule over the Temple and thus, by definition, the Temple hierarchy. See Josephus, *Jewish Antiquities* 13.366, and the Dead Sea Scroll 1QS28a, 2.3–7; cf. also D. Daube, 'Three Notes Having To Do With Johanan ben Zaccai', *Journal of Theological Studies*, 11 (1960), pp. 53–62.

25 On John and the Essenes, see Thiede, *The Dead Sea Scrolls and the Jewish Origins of Christianity*, pp. 190–1; cf. Josephus, *Jewish War* 2.128, 2.140–50, and the Dead Sea Scrolls 1QS3.9, CD 10.11.

26 Followers of the Baptist existed, as a Jewish sect, well into early Christianity (Acts 19.1–7) and post-New Testament times; the 'Mandaeans', who can still be found in southern Iraq, probably originated as a Johannine baptismal movement.

27 For Jews, the Bible, the *Tanakh*, ends with 2 Chronicles, the last of the third part of the Bible, the 'Ketubim' ('writings'). Malachi is the last of the texts in the second part, the 'Nebi'im' or 'prophets', and it is the last of the 'Tree Asar', the 'Twelve Minor Prophets'.

28 For reasons that are obscure, all the standard translations omit this decisive first word.

29 Matthew 5.35 (Lamentations 2.1); Matthew 5.39 (Lamentations 3.30).

30 See Josephus, *Jewish Antiquities* 18.28.

31 Such variations occur frequently in the Bible, as they do today. It will be interesting to find out one day whether historians will call the former US President Clinton by the name William or Bill, and the British Prime Minister Blair by Anthony or Tony. Some manuscripts of the Greek Bible have the shorter variant in 1 Chronicles 26.3 and 1 Esdras 9.1, 23.

32 Cf., for example, Luke 1.59–64.

33 Aristophanes, *The Clouds* 351.

34 See M. L. Lang, *Socrates in the Agora*, American School of Classical Studies at Athens, no. 17 (Princeton: 1978), p. 13.

35 For the papyrus, dated to 416 BC, see E. G. Kraehling (ed.), *The Brooklyn Museum Aramaic Papyri: New Documents of the Fifth Century BC from the Jewish Colony of Elephantine* (New Haven: 1953), pp. 224–31, plate VIII. Cf. J. A. Fitzmyer, 'Aramaic "Kephâ" and Peter's Name in the New Testament', in J. A. Fitzmyer, *To Advance the Gospel* (New York: 1981), pp. 112–24.

36 See J. H. Charlesworth, 'Has the Name "Peter" Been Found among the Dead Sea Scrolls?', in B. Mayer (ed.), *Christen und Christliches in Qumran?* (Regensburg: 1992), pp. 213–25. The Aramaic 'kêphâ' is documented in several other scrolls, e.g. 11QtgJob32.1; 33.9.

37 Still the most circumspect analysis of the debate, twenty years after its first publication, and from a Protestant point of view, is G. Maier, 'The Church in the Gospel of Matthew: Hermeneutical Analysis of the Current Debate', in D. A. Carson (ed.), *Biblical Interpretation and the Church: Text and Context* (Exeter: 1984), pp. 45–63. See also the Anglican comment of R. T. France in his *The Gospel According to Matthew: An Introduction and Commentary* (Leicester and Grand Rapids: 1985), p. 254: 'It is only Protestant overreaction to the Roman Catholic claim (which of course has no foundation in the text) that what here is said of Peter applies also to the later bishops of Rome, that has led some to claim that the "rock" here is not Peter at all but the faith which he has just confessed. . . . Of course it is on the basis of Peter's confession that Jesus declares his role as the church's foundation, but it is to Peter, not to his confession, that the rock metaphor is applied.'

38 See, for example, Thucydides, *History of the Peloponnesian War* 2.22; Plato, *Gorgias*, 456b.

39 See, for example, 1QM4.10, and cf. the Community Rule 1QS8.6–8, an interpretation of Isaiah 28.16, about the council of the community which will stand fast in the last days, like a rock which cannot waver.

40 Cf. Psalm 9.13, 107.18; Wisdom of Solomon 16.13; etc.

5 Life after Death? Charon's Coin and Boxes for Bones in Jerusalem

1 Cf. W. Reinhardt, 'The Population Size of Jerusalem and the Numerical Growth of the Jerusalem Church', in R. Bauckham (ed.), *The Book of Acts in its First Century Setting*, vol. 4: *The Book of Acts in its Palestinian Setting* (Grand Rapids and Carlisle: 1995), pp. 258–65.

2 Megillah 7b. On Esther's controversial role in orthodox Judaism at the time of Jesus, see Thiede, *The Dead Sea Scrolls and the Jewish Origins of Christianity*, pp. 105–23.

3 First published by R. Weill, *La Cité de David. Compte rendu des fouilles executées à Jérusalem, sur le site de la ville primitive. Campagne de 1913–1914* (Paris: 1920), vol. 1, p. 30; vol. 2, plate 25a (photo). Recent investigations have confirmed, beyond reasonable doubt, a date prior to the destruction of the Temple in AD 70. See, among others, the summary in R. Reich, 'The Synagogue and the *mikveh* in Eretz-Israel in the Second Temple, Mishnaic, and Talmudic Periods', in D. Urman and P. V. M. Flesher (eds), *Ancient Synagogues: Historical Analysis and Archaeological Discovery* (Leiden: 1994), vol. 1, pp. 289–97.

4 Mark obviously presupposes that at least some of his readers knew Rufus and Alexander as fellow-Christians.

5 In the New Testament, see Acts 10.2 (Cornelius); Acts 16.14 (Lydia), etc.; cf. Josephus, *Jewish Antiquities* 14.110; 19.195 (Nero's wife Poppaea).

6 See also Josephus, *Jewish Antiquities* 15.417. Cf. P. Segal, 'The Penalty of the Warning Inscription from the Temple of Jerusalem', *Israel Exploration Journal*, 39 (1989), pp. 79–84; for photos of both inscriptions, see A. Millard, *Discoveries from the Time of Jesus* (Oxford: 1990), p. 83.

7 Mark (15.26) and Matthew (27.37) use the correct Greek technical term for the Latin 'causa poenae': 'aitía' (cf. John 19.4, 6; Acts 13.28, 23.28, 28.18). For a discussion of the legal and technical details, see Thiede and d'Ancona, *The Quest for the True Cross*, pp. 78–90.

8 The order of the three languages in modern editions of the Greek New Testament and most recent translations, Hebrew–Latin–Greek, is based on text-critical decisions. Readers of the Authorized Version, the 'King James Bible', still find 'and it was written in Hebrew, and Greek, and Latin'. It is also the sequence of the Latin Vulgate, although the 'Neo-Vulgate', which is a modern edition of the Latin text, copies the altered Greek sequence. It is of no use whatsoever to students of the New Testament and its transmission in Latin and should therefore be avoided (it is this useless 'Neo-Vulgate' which is printed with the Greek text in the current standard edition, Nestle–Aland, *Novum Testamentum Graece et Latine*). Most of the oldest manuscripts, beginning with the papyrus P66 of *c.* AD 150 and the Codices Sinaiticus and Vaticanus, offer

Hebrew–Latin–Greek, whereas Hebrew–Greek–Latin can be found in the Codex Alexandrinus, several later codices, most minuscules and the Old Latin tradition. The editorial reason given for the reading Hebrew–Latin–Greek is strange, to say the least: apart from the manuscript evidence, which is, as we have seen, ambiguous, this is the order of 'the national language, the official language, the common language'. And the alternative sequel is explained as 'a secondary development, with the languages arranged in accord with a geographical order going from East to West' – a completely anachronistic statement (Metzger, *A Textual Commentary on the Greek New Testament*, p. 217). Applying socio-political logic, we should assume the following order: Hebrew – the language of the Temple and thus the religious language of the alleged 'King of the Jews'; Greek – the language understood by all pilgrims, all Romans and all locals; and finally, Latin – the formal language of the Roman administration, sealing, as it were, this Roman document. Thus, the sequence of the Codex Alexandrinus etc., and of the old Vulgate, looks much more plausible. There now also exists epigraphic evidence: the recently authenticated fragment of the headboard at Santa Croce in Gerusalemme, Rome, has Hebrew–Greek–Latin. (See Thiede and d'Ancona, *The Quest for the True Cross*, pp. 71–107.) Interestingly, most manuscripts of Luke's Gospel also mention the three languages (23.38), albeit in a different order which cannot have been copied from John: Greek–Latin–Hebrew (to be found in the original, uncorrected Codex Sinaiticus, the Codices Alexandrinus and Bezae, and numerous minuscules). This still is the English text of the Authorized Version.

9 Josephus, *Jewish Antiquities* 18.116–99.
10 *Proto-Gospel of James* 23. The year of the birth of John was 8 BC; Jesus was born in early 7 BC, around 6 January; Herod died in 4 BC. These dates are not the Gospels' fault, but were caused by the erroneous calendar reform of Dionysius Exiguus (*c.* AD 478–535), on behalf of Pope John I. In two of his writings, *De cyclo magno Paschale* and *Argumenta paschalia*, both *c.* AD 526–32, he invented the year '0', miscalculated his starting point, the foundation of Rome, and ended up seven years late. For the most up to date and detailed analysis, see K. Ferrari d'Occhieppo, *Der Stern von Bethlehem in astronomischer Sicht*.

11 Press reports apart, an interim analysis was published by J. E. Zias and E. Puech, 'Le Tombeau de Zacharie et Siméon au monument funéraire dit d'Absalom dans la Vallée de Josaphat', *Revue Biblique*, 110:3 (2003), pp. 321–35. A further report was presented by Zias at the annual meeting of the American Schools of Oriental Research in Atlanta in November 2003.

12 Theodosius, *De situ terrae sanctae* 9.

13 As the inscription clearly follows the text of the Sinaiticus, over against variant readings in other manuscripts, and since it offers – unlike the papyri and codices of the New Testament – an indisputable location, the textual evidence from the tomb will have to be studied by those classical philologists who analyse the origin and distribution of New Testament types of text, and the scribal variants.

14 In 1960 and 1972, two Greek inscriptions with Romans 13.3 were found at Caesarea Maritima. Dated to the late fourth/early fifth century, they are part of some floor mosaics and may have belonged to the archives of the Praetorium. In 1982, a fifth-/sixth-century mosaic with the Greek text of 1 Corinthians 15.52–3 was found in a burial cave near the Khirbet ed-Deir monastery east of Hebron.

15 See also Josephus, *Jewish Antiquities* 18.16.

16 4Q521, fr. 4, 11–12. Cf. Thiede, *The Dead Sea Scrolls and the Jewish Origins of Christianity*, pp. 204–9. 4Q521 was published in 1992 and surprised those who had not found any specific allusions to such an Essene belief in Philo and Josephus. But it seems that Hippolytus (*c.* AD 170–236) still knew about it: the teaching of the resurrection, Hippolytus wrote in his *Against all heresies* 9.27, had found support among the Essenes, 'for they acknowledge both that the flesh will rise again, and that it will be immortal'.

17 Babylonian Talmud, Ebel Rabbati (= the great one on mourning, euphemistically called 'Semakhot', 'rejoicings', in some sources), 13.

18 Sanhedrin 6.6 (cf. 46b, 47b).

19 See N. Haas, 'Anthropological Observations on the Skeletal Remains from Giv'at ha-Mivtar', *Israel Exploration Journal*, 20 (1970), pp. 38–59; and above all, J. Zias and E. Sekeles, 'The Crucified Man from Giv'at ha-Mivtar: A Reappraisal', *Israel Exploration Journal*, 35 (1985), pp. 22–7. The *clavus trabalis* was used for beams – see Horace, *Carmina* 1.35.18, and became

idiomatic: 'trabali clavo figere' meant 'to nail it down' (Cicero, *In Verrem* 5.53).

20 As so often with discoveries of that period (and all too often even today), the first publication was late and provisional. After a brief note by Sukenik in the *Bulletin of the American Schools of Oriental Research*, 88 (1942), p. 38, it took his former assistant Avigad twenty years to publish 'A Depository of Inscribed Ossuaries in the Kidron Valley', in *Israel Exploration Journal*, 12 (1962), pp. 1–12.

21 After the letters 'QRNY', there is a superfluous 'T' (the final letter of the Hebrew alphabet, 'taw'). This has puzzled scholars, but it probably means nothing more than a conclusion to the text. For the uses of 'taw' in Hebrew inscriptions as a symbol of deliverance and even as a cryptogram for the name of God, cf. J. Finegan, *The Archaeology of the New Testament: The Life of Jesus and the Beginning of the Early Church* (rev. edn Princeton: 1992), pp. 346–8.

22 In a different tomb, discovered at the church of 'Dominus flevit' on the Mount of Olives, yet another man from this part of the Roman Empire was buried in an ossuary: 'Philōn Kyrēnaīos', 'Philon the Cyrenian'; see P. B. Bagatti and J. T. Milik, *Gli scavi del 'Dominus flevit' (Monte Oliveto-Gerusalemme)* (Jerusalem: 1958), p. 81.

23 See J. Zias, 'Ossuario col nome di Alessandro, figlio di Simone di Cirene', in A. Donati (ed.), *Dalla Terra alle Genti. La diffusione del cristianesimo nei primi secoli* (exhibition catalogue, Rimini, 31 March–1 September 1996; Milan: 1996), p. 167.

24 Cf. T. Ilan, *Lexicon of Jewish Names in Antiquity*, vol. 1, (Tuebingen: 2002).

25 F. F. Bruce, *The Letter of Paul to the Romans: An Introduction and Commentary* (Leicester and Grand Rapids: 1985), pp. 260–1.

26 The latest constructive contribution by a New Testament scholar was published as Grove Book B30: P. Head, *Is the New Testament Reliable?* (Cambridge: 2003). For a classical philologist's position, see U. Victor, 'Was ein Texthistoriker zur Entstehung der Evangelien sagen kann', *Biblica*, 79 (1998), pp. 499–513, and 'Einleitung', in Victor *et al.* (eds), *Antike Kultur und Neues Testament*, pp. 13–29.

27 For a detailed list and discussion of such references, see still F. F. Bruce, *Jesus and Christian Origins Outside the New Testament* (London: 1974).

28 This is not the place to discuss the meaning of 'brothers' and 'sisters'. Philologically, the Greek words *adelphoi* and *adelphai* mean precisely that; but it seems plausible that Jesus' siblings were children from a first marriage of Joseph, who married Mary later after becoming a widower. Legally, this would have made Jesus their brother; there is no Jewish or Greek term for 'half-brother' or '-sister', nor for 'adoptive son'. The notion of a widower Joseph, with children from his first marriage, was first recorded in the *Proto-Gospel of James* 17.1; cf. also Gregory of Nyssa (*c.* AD 330–395), *In Christi Resurrectionem*, II. This remains the position of all orthodox and catholic churches with the exception of the Roman Catholic church, which later taught that 'brothers' and 'sisters' means 'cousins', children of the other Mary mentioned in Mark 15.40. This philological and text-critical implausibility was first mooted by Jerome, in his polemical treatise of AD 383, 'Adversus Helvidium de Mariae virginitate perpetua'. See R. Bauckham, *Jude and the Relatives of Jesus in the Early Church* (Edinburgh: 1990), pp. 19–32.

29 According to R. Hachlili, *Names and Nicknames of Jews in Second Temple Times* (Jerusalem: 1984), Joseph was second (after Simon), Jesus varied between third and sixth place, and James was ninth to twelfth. Given the incomplete archaeological data from that period, certainty on such matters is impossible, but at least we have a rough idea of how popular these names were.

30 Josephus, *Jewish Antiquities* 20.200.

31 H. Shanks and B. Witherington III, *The Brother of Jesus. The Dramatic Story & Meaning of the First Archaeological Link to Jesus and His Family* (London and New York: 2003). Hershel Shanks is the editor of the *Biblical Archaeology Review*; Ben Witherington III is a respected New Testament scholar teaching at Asbury Theological Seminary in Lexington, Kentucky. Fortunately for his reputation, his contribution to the book, part II, 'The Story of James, Son of Joseph, Brother of Jesus' (pp. 89–209), does not depend on the existence of the ossuary at all (he hardly ever refers to it) and is a brief but useful introduction to the role of James in the early Church.

32 Ironically, it was a Jewish scholar at Bar Ilan University, Professor Daniel R. Schwartz, who defended the trustworthiness of Luke over

against Josephus in his *Agrippa I: The Last King of Judaea* (Tuebingen: 1990), pp. 208–16, etc.

33 Israel Antiquities Authority, Jerusalem, press conference and press release of 18 June 2003.

34 *Haaretz*, 25 July 2003, with photos. In the meantime, Oded Golan's network of forgeries has been exposed in a TV documentary, 'The History Merchants: Oded Golan – Another Type of Na'aman Ocher ("Trustworthy")', Israel Television, Channel 2, 18 February 2004. The documentary also exposes the vested interests of the French epigrapher André Lemaire, the gullibility of the *Biblical Archaeology Review* and the strategies of its editor, Hershel Shanks.

35 Hegesippus (*c.* AD 120–190), *Hypomnemata*, quoted in Eusebius, *Church History* 2.23.5–7. Hegesippus was a Jewish-Christian writer and a native Greek-speaker from the eastern Roman Empire, with access to local traditions. In *c.* AD 160 he travelled to Rome, to study the apostolic traditions in the capital. The reference to 'the prophets' probably means Isaiah 3.10 in the Septuagint, which Hegesippus may have seen as a prophecy of the murder of James 'the Just'/'the Righteous' (*dikaios* in Greek): 'Woe to their soul, for they have devised an evil counsel against themselves, saying against themselves: "Let us bind the Righteous/the Just, for he is burdensome to us; therefore they shall eat the fruits of their works."' Later in his account of the killing of James, he quotes the verse explicitly (Eusebius, *Church History* 2.23.15).

36 On their cultural background in Galilee and Jerusalem, see M. Hengel, *The 'Hellenization' of Judaea in the First Century after Christ* (London and Philadelphia: 1989). For Jerusalem in particular, see M. Hengel, The *Pre-Christian Paul* (London and Philadelphia: 1991), pp. 54–62, 68–9. The classical papyrologist C. H. Roberts rightly saw the broader picture: the world into which Christianity was born 'was, if not literary, literate to a remarkable degree; in the Near East in the first century of our era writing was an essential accompaniment of life at almost all levels to an extent without parallel in living memory. In the New Testament, reading is not an unusual accomplishment' (C. H. Roberts, 'Books in the Graeco-Roman World and in the New Testament', in P. R. Ackroyd and C. F. Evans (eds), *The Cambridge History of the Bible*, vol. 1 (Cambridge: 1970), p. 48.

37 Unfortunately, quite a few New Testament scholars still subscribe to the naive idea that this speech, like most other speeches in Acts, is basically Luke's creation. The use of linguistic nuances and rhetorics betrays the typical traces of each individual, and while Luke condensed his material rather than producing an early Christian Hansard, he left the individual character unmanipulated.

38 Paul's animosity towards these people and to Peter's diplomatic flexibility is understandable enough. As the 'Apostle to the Gentiles', he was loath to see anyone advocating the equal rights of Jewish Christians in his immediate vicinity, all the more as he thought he had won Peter over to his case. The fact, admitted by Paul himself, that the Antioch 'veteran' Barnabas sided with Peter in this conflict of interests points to a rather more complex situation, and Paul's admirable learning curve can be seen in his later first letter to the Corinthians, 9.19–23, where he adopts Peter's position. Tertullian acknowledged this as early as *c.* AD 190, in his *Against Marcion* 1.20; cf. also J. D. G. Dunn, *Unity and Diversity in the New Testament* (London: 1977), pp. 252–4.

39 The tradition, still defended by some, that Matthew originally wrote his gospel in Aramaic is based on a misunderstanding of Papias, who claimed, in *c.* AD 110, that Matthew was the first to write down the *lógia*, the sayings, of the Lord and did so 'Hebraïdi dialektō', in the Aramaic language, and that 'everyone interpreted them as best he could' (quoted in Eusebius, *Church History* 3.39.16). Papias is thus referring to a collection of utterances, perhaps whole sermons, which Levi-Matthew, the disciple, had protocolled in the original Aramaic. There is no talk of a completed Gospel with extended narrative passages.

40 See, among others, P. H. Davids, *The Epistle of James: A Commentary on the Greek Text* (Exeter: 1982), pp. 2–22; R. Bauckham, *Jude and the Relatives of Jesus on the Early Church* (Edinburgh: 1990), pp. 128–33; D. Guthrie, *New Testament Introduction*, 4th edn (Leicester: 1990), pp. 722–53; Carson *et al.*, *An Introduction to the New Testament*, pp. 409–20. After a detailed study of the linguistic and cultural, theological and allegedly anti-Pauline pros and cons, Carson *et al.* sum up: 'We conclude, then, that James the brother of the Lord is the author of the letter. This is the natural implication of the letter's own claims, and it has no deci-

sive argument against it' (p. 413). It should also be noted that J. N. Sevenster's mould-breaking study of 1968, *'Do You Know Greek?' How Much Greek Could the First Jewish Christians Have Known?* (Leiden: 1968), uses the letter of James as one of his test cases and concludes that on linguistic grounds alone, the Lord's brother could very well have written it (p. 191).

41 The Damascus Document CD 7.16 and the Florilegium 4QFlor1.10–13. Cf. Thiede, *The Dead Sea Scrolls and the Jewish Origins of Christianity*, pp. 214–20.

42 First recognized correctly by O. Cullmann, 'The Significance of the Qumran Texts for Research into the Beginnings of Christianity', *Journal of Biblical Literature*, 74 (1955), pp. 213–26. See also B. Pixner, *Wege des Messias und Staetten der Urkirche*, 3rd augm. edn (Giessen: 1996), pp. 333–4, 367–9, 386–7, with further literature.

43 On his dialogue in Greek with the Syrophoenician woman, and on the meaning of the site at Caesarea Philippi, see Chapter 4 above; cf. also Matthew 28.19–20 and Acts 1.8, two statements which have often been relegated to the scrapheap of ideological scholarship, but which should be taken seriously as authentic information.

44 Z. Greenhut, 'Discovery of the Caiaphas Family Tomb', *Jerusalem Perspective*, 4 (July–October 1991), pp. 6–12, and 'The "Caiaphas" Tomb in North Talpiot', *Atiqot*, 21 (1992), pp. 63–71.

45 See R. Reich, 'Ossuary Inscriptions from the Caiaphas Tomb', *Jerusalem Perspective*, 4 (July–October 1991), pp. 13–22, and 'Caiaphas' Name Inscribed on Bone Boxes', *Biblical Archaeology Review*, 18:5 (1992), pp. 38–44. A philologically and epigraphically erroneous attempt to refute the analysis of the experts was published by W. Horbury, 'The "Caiaphas" Ossuaries and Joseph Caiaphas', *Palestine Exploration Quarterly*, 126 (1994), pp. 32–48.

46 Josephus, *Jewish Antiquities* 18.35: 'Iōsēpos ho Kaïaphas'; *Jewish Antiquities* 18.95: 'Iōsēpon ton Kaïaphan epikaloumenon'. 'Caiaphas' is an epithet or byname; literally it means 'basket-bearer'. Jewish and Roman nomenclature often used bynames to distinguish family members, or different branches of a family – thus 'Peter/Kephas' was a byname of Simon, the son of Jonah, and 'Tacitus' was a byname of the famous historian whose first name was Publius, and whose family name was Cornelius (which means that the first non-Jew baptized by Peter, the centurion Cornelius at Caesarea

Maritima, belonged to the same *gens* or family as, several decades later, the historian Tacitus). Likewise, the Roman prefect Pontius Pilate, whose first name is unknown, was a member of the Pontius family and belonged to a branch called the 'Pilatii' or 'spear-bearers'.

47 For an anthropological analysis of the bones in both ossuaries, and the probability of the high priest's bones in the one marked 'Joseph Bar Caiaphas', see J. Zias, 'Human Skeletal Remains from the 'Caiaphas' Tomb', *Atiqot*, 21 (1992), pp. 78–80.

48 Acts 12.21–3; Josephus, *Jewish Antiquities* 19.346–51.

49 The myth is told in several variations: sometimes the river is the Acheron or it is the lake Acherusia. On the changing meanings of 'Hades', which cannot simply be equated with our 'hell', see J. M. C. Toynbee, *Death and Burial in the Roman World* (London: 1971); D. C. Kurtz and J. Boardman, *Greek Burial Customs* (London: 1971).

50 R. Hachlili and A. Killebrew, 'Jewish Funerary Customs during the Second Temple Period in the Light of Excavations in the Jericho Necropolis', *Palestine Exploration Quarterly*, 115 (1983), pp. 109–32.

51 L. Y. Rahmani, 'Jason's Tomb', *Israel Exploration Journal*, 17 (1967), pp. 61–100.

52 Josephus, *Jewish Antiquities* 19.355–8.

53 Josephus, *Jewish War* 2.175–7.

54 Caiaphas' complicity follows from the timing of such events. His name hardly ever appears in the ancient sources; even Mark only calls him 'the high priest'. Cf. V. Eppstein, 'The Historicity of the Gospel Account of the Cleansing of the Temple', *Zeitschrift fuer die neutestamentliche Wissenschaft*, 55 (1964), pp. 42–58. For Simon ben Gamaliel, see the Talmud, Keritot 1.7.

55 Josephus, *Jewish Antiquities* 18.90–5.

56 Talmud, Pesachim 54a. The 'House of Hannas' (cf. Luke 3.2; Acts 4.6) is mentioned by name; Hannas was Caiaphas' father-in-law (John 18.13, 24). It has even been suggested by Jewish scholars that Caiaphas may have survived in office under two prefects for a record-breaking period, because he bribed them. Cf. J. Klausner, *Jesus of Nazareth* (London: 1925), p. 217 (originally published in Hebrew, *Jeshu Ha-Nozri* (Jerusalem: 1922)); Ch. Cohn, *The Trial*

and Death of Jesus (New York: 1977), pp. 50–1; Talmud, Yoma 8b; cf. Sifre Bamidbar 131.

6 Back to the Sources: Bookshops, Libraries and Messengers

1 Pliny the Elder, *Natural History* 13.70.

2 Although we do not have any reliable information on Haftara portions used in synagogues before the destruction of the Temple in AD 70 and the ensuing reorganization of worship, the portion of the Torah which someone else would have read in the synagogue that day probably was Leviticus 25.1—27.34, which includes 25.10, the verse quoted and expanded in Isaiah 61.2.

3 The Greek word *titlos* is derived from the Latin *titulus*. John therefore corroborates the assumption that the usage was introduced by the Romans, together with the administrative terminology in Latin. For further details and literature, see Thiede and d'Ancona, *The Quest for the True Cross*.

4 Cf. Thiede and d'Ancona, *The Quest for the True Cross*, pp. 78–81.

5 Cf., for example, E. R. Richards, *The Secretary in the Letters of Paul* (Tuebingen: 1991).

6 The most detailed study, putting paid to theories of acceptable pseudepigraphy in early Christianity, is A. D. Baum, *Pseudepigraphie und literarische Faelschung im fruehen Christentum* (Tuebingen: 2001).

7 'kalamos grammateōs oxygraphou'. On Greek shorthand writing among Jews in the third/second century BC and after, see Richards, *The Secretary in the Letters of Paul*, pp. 28–43; cf. Thiede, *The Dead Sea Scrolls and the Jewish Origins of Christianity*, pp. 80–3.

8 Pliny the Elder, *Natural History* 16.157; Martial, *Epigrams* 14.38.

9 Suetonius, *Divus Iulius* 56.6.

10 Horace, *De arte poetica* 386–90.

11 Persius, *Satires* 3.10–11. Persius was expert enough to distinguish between the 'hair' and 'flesh' sides of a parchment.

12 An evaluation first made by C. H. Roberts and T. C. Skeat, *The Birth of the Codex* (London: 1983), p. 22. Refreshingly, Roberts and Skeat, papyrologists and classical philologists by training and trade, are rightly adamant that the letter was written by Paul, and thus in the first century. For the most plausible date, *c.* AD 63/4, and for Paul

as its author, see the painstakingly detailed analysis by W. D.
Mounce in his circumspect commentary: *Pastoral Epistles*, Word
Biblical Commentary vol. 46 (Nashville: 2000), pp. xli–cxxix.

13 The first to notice the real meaning of *phailonēs* was John
Chrysostom (*c.* AD 349–407), *Homilies* 10. Cf. the Syriac 'Peshitta'
of 2 Timothy 4.13 ('protective cover'); see also Th. Birt, *Das antike
Buchwesen in seinem Verhaeltnis zur Literatur* (repr. Darmstadt:
1974), pp. 65, 88–9; W. Lock, *Godliness and Contentment: Studies
in the Three Pastoral Epistles* (Grand Rapids: 1982), p. 118.

14 Martial, *Epigrams* 13.1.1–2.

15 Many scholars still believe that Christian scribes never used scrolls,
but began with the codex straight away. This is not substantiated by
the evidence. The change from scroll to codex took place very early,
probably in the late sixties and seventies of the first century, but the
New Testament writings presuppose scrolls in the apostolic period
(see Revelation 5.1 and 6.14 above), and early Christian literature
and art (catacomb frescos) confirm this practice. For a date prior to
AD 70, cf. also Roberts and Skeat, *The Birth of the Codex*, pp. 58–9.
See also C. P. Thiede, 'On the Development of Scroll and Codex in
the Early Church', in his *Rekindling the Word: In Search of Gospel
Truth* (Leominster and Valley Forge, Pa.: 1995), pp. 84–92; C. P.
Thiede, 'Papyrologie', in Victor *et al.* (eds), *Antike Kultur und Neues
Testament*, pp. 50–5, with further literature. Christians continued to
use the old scrolls until they fell apart, while new copies were written in the codex format. A fresco in the Roman Domitilla Catacombs
faithfully preserves this tradition. Painted in the third century, it
shows the martyr Petronilla, who died in AD 96. Above her left shoul-
der, there is an opened codex – this is what she and other Christians
had in the nineties. But at her feet, there is a *capsa*, a container for
scrolls, with several scrolls inside.

16 We do not know what Luke collected and consulted. If Papias, the
bishop of Hierapolis who, in *c.* AD 110, mentioned an Aramaic collection of sayings (*logia*) written down by Levi-Matthew (see
Eusebius, *Church History* 3.39.15), was right, even such an Aramaic
text, compiled by an eyewitness disciple, could have been among
Luke's sources.

17 Papyrus Vindobonensis Sijpenstein 26, part of a correspondence
between two low-ranking civil servants. Cf. H. Koskenniemi,

Studien zur Idee und Phraseologie des griechischen Briefes (Helsinki: 1956), p. 162.

18 Cf. C. W. Griggs, *Early Egyptian Christianity: From its Origins to 451 C.E.* (2nd edn Leiden: 1991).

19 Photos, Greek text, Italian translation, with commentary and an analysis of the Christian Greek vocabulary, in I. Ramelli, 'Una delle più antiche lettere cristiane extracanoniche?', Aegyptus, 80 (2000), pp. 169–88. On the palaeography and dating, see also O. Montevecchi, 'THN ΕΠΙΣΤΟΛΗΝ ΚΕΧΙΑΣΜΕΝΗΝ', *Aegyptus*, 80 (2000), pp. 189–94.

20 'Letter of Aristeas' 9–11, etc. The letter, its historical background and the role of Demetrius are discussed in R. Blum, *Kallimachos: The Alexandrian Library and the Origins of Bibliography* (Madison: 1991), pp. 100–2; see also Stone, *Jewish Writings of the Second Temple Period*, pp. 75–80.

21 Exact figures have not survived. Aulus Gellius, the second-century author of the Latin *Attic Nights*, mentions 700,000 scrolls (*Attic Nights* 7.13.3); Ammianus Marcellinus (*c.* AD 330–400) insists on the 'unanimous trustworthiness' of the ancient sources about the 700,000 scrolls which were burnt during Caesar's naval attack on the city in 47 BC (*Roman History* 25.16.13). John Tzetzes, a Byzantine monk (*c.* 1110–1180), alludes to unknown sources according to which the 'Museion' housed 490,000 scrolls, and the 'Serapeion' another 42,800 (for Tzetzes' text, see G. Kaibel (ed.), *Comicorum Graecorum Fragmenta* (Berlin: 1899), pp. 17–33). Cf. E. A. Parsons, *The Alexandrian Library* (London: 1952), pp. 106–121; Blum, *Kallimachos*, pp. 104–13. See also L. Casson, *Libraries in the Ancient World* (New Haven and London: 2001), pp. 31–47, which confirms Tzetzes' estimate.

22 On the date of *Octavius* and the allusions to the Old and New Testament and non-biblical writings, see C. P. Thiede, 'A Pagan Reader of 2 Peter: Cosmic Conflagration in 2 Peter 3 and the *Octavius* of Minucius Felix', *Journal for the Study of the New Testament*, 26 (1986), pp. 79–96.

23 Minucius Felix, *Octavius* 39.1.

24 Cf. H. Y. Gamble, *Books and Readers in the Early Church: A History of Early Christian Texts* (New Haven and London: 1995), pp. 144–202.

25 N. Orme, review of Stephen Miller and Robert Huber *The Bible: A History* (Oxford: 2003), in *Church Times*, 16 May 2003, p. 22. Orme also asked why so many scholars assume that the Gospels should be dated to the late first century, against the fact that they do not even reflect, clearly and unmistakably, the destruction of Jerusalem and the Temple in AD 70.

26 But see, on the evidence of Gospel publishing prior to Paul's letters, P. E. Hughes, *The Second Epistle to the Corinthians*, 2nd edn (Grand Rapids: 1986), pp. 311–16, discussing 2 Corinthians 8.18 as a reference to Luke's Gospel ('ton adelphon hou ho epainos en tō euangeliō' , 'because of the gospel', not, as in most modern translations, because of his proclamation of the gospel, or his service to the gospel). Early Church fathers saw Luke in this reference; see also J. Wenham, *Redating Matthew, Mark, and Luke: A Fresh Assault on the Synoptic Problem* (London: 1991), pp. 207–9, 230–8; H. Riesenfeld, 'Neues Licht auf die Entstehung der Evangelien: Handschriften vom Toten Meer und andere Indizien', in B. Mayer (ed.), *Christen und Christliches in Qumran?* (Regensburg: 1992), pp. 182 *et al.* The use of *Euangélion* for a specific genre of literature can also be found in two of the earliest writings of post-New Testament literature, the letters of Ignatius (martyred *c.* AD 109) to the Smyrnaeans and to the Philadelphians. In *Smyrneans*, he describes those who deny Christ and writes: 'The words of the prophets did not convince them, nor the law of Moses, nor, so far, the Gospel' (5.1); see also 7.5 and *Philadelphians* 8.2. From quotes and allusions in his letters, it transpires that his favourite Gospel was Matthew, closely followed by John. For a characteristic summary and defence of the current majority position, which prefers a much later date for the introduction of 'Gospel' as a technical term for a book about Jesus, see J. A. Kelhoffer, '"How Soon a Book" Revisited: ΕΥΑΓΓΣΛΙΟΝ as a Reference to "Gospel" Materials in the First Half of the Second Century', *Zeitschrift fuer die neutestamentliche Wissenschaft*, 95 (2004), pp. 1–34.

27 AD 40 is the date suggested by a Jewish expert in Hellenistic literature, Guenther Zuntz (Professor of Hellenistic Greek at Manchester University): 'Wann wurde das Evangelium Marci geschrieben?', in H. Cancik (ed.), *Markus-Philologie* (Tuebingen: 1984), pp. 47–71. For a date in the forties of the first century, see also J. A. T.

Robinson, *Redating the New Testament* (London: 1976), B. Orchard and H. Riley, *The Order of the Synoptics* (Macon, Ga.: 1987), Wenham, *Redating Matthew, Mark, and Luke*; C. P. Thiede and M. d'Ancona, *The Jesus Papyrus* (London: 1996). For a summary of the traditional arguments for and against a date in the forties, see Guthrie, *New Testament Introduction*, pp. 81–9.

28 See also Thiede, *The Dead Sea Scrolls and the Jewish Origins of Christianity*, pp. 124–81.

29 On the date, the most circumspect analysis is still F. Manns, *John and Jamnia: How the Break Occurred Between Jews and Christians* (Jerusalem: 1988), above all pp. 15–30.

30 At Jamnia, the process of determining the books of the 'Old Testament' as we still have them in Hebrew Bibles today was initiated – resulting in a canon without the 'Apocrypha' of the Greek tradition, and books like Ezekiel and the Song of Songs being included only after lengthy discussions, while the popular Ben Sirach was excluded. See the account in the Talmud, Tosefta Yadaim.

31 This additional benediction was widespread and even reached Cairo, where an early medieval copy was found in the *genizah* of the Ben-Ezra Synagogue. Cf. W. Bacher, *Die Agada der Tannaiten* (Strasbourg: 1903), vol. 1, pp. 370–2.

32 The Jewish scholar Richard L. Rubinstein called it a family dispute within Judaism: see R. L. Rubinstein, *My Brother Paul* (New York: 1972), p. 115.

33 See C. P. Thiede and U. Stingelin, *Die Wurzeln des Antisemitismus: Judenfeindschaft in der Antike, im frühen Christentum und im Koran* 5th edn (Basel: 2003), with further literature.

34 See Y. Yadin, 'The Excavation of Masada – 1963/64: Preliminary Report', in *Israel Exploration Journal*, 15 (1965), pp. 1–120; and *Masada: Herod's Fortress and the Zealots' Last Stand* (London: 1966).

35 See C. Newsom, *Songs of the Sabbath Sacrifice: A Critical Edition* (Atlanta: 1985), Masada fragment 1039–200. Numerous fragments of this text were also found at Qumran: 4Q400–4Q407 and 11Q17. Many scholars assume that the synagogal library was in fact a *genizah*, a storage room for disused scrolls which were not thrown away but were collected and buried or burnt. But even a *genizah*

presupposes the prior existence of a library from which the scrolls were taken.

36 For the Jewish Greek texts and the Latin documents left behind by the occupying Romans, see H. M. Cotton and J. Geiger (eds), *Masada II: The Latin and Greek Documents* (Jerusalem: 1989).

37 Unpublished remarks by Professor Talmon in the public debate during the Dead Sea Scrolls Conference at the Notre Dame Centre Jerusalem, 3 January 1999. Recently, E. Puech and E. Muro have tried to link 7Q4 with passages from *Enoch*, but using their method and checking the original fragments, the result is in fact the opposite: five new fragments from 1 Timothy have come to light. Another fragment, 7Q19, appears to be a lost commentary on Paul's letter to the Romans. For a detailed description of the procedure and all aspects of the debate about Cave 7, its jar and its papyri, see Thiede, *The Dead Sea Scrolls and the Jewish Origins of Christianity*, pp. 124–81, 237–44.

38 For a more general treatment of Jewish reticence in these matters, see M. Goodman, 'Jewish Proselytizing in the First Century', in J. Lieu, J. North and T. Rajak (eds), *The Jews among Pagans and Christians in the Roman Empire*, 2nd edn (London and New York: 1994), pp. 55–78.

39 Cf. Th. Birt, *Das antike Buchwesen in seinem Verhæltnis zur Literatur* (repr. Aalen: 1974), pp. 342–64, 430–7; H. Blanck, *Das Buch in der Antike* (Munich: 1992), pp. 113–78. See also Casson, *Libraries in the Ancient World*.

40 Martial, *Epigrams* 1.2.

41 On general access to city libraries, see W. Clarysse and K. Vandorpe, *Boeken en Bibliotheken in de Oudheid* (Leuven: 1996), pp. 74–87; Blanck, *Das Buch in der Antike*, pp. 133–52; cf. Casson, *Libraries in the Ancient World*, pp. 48–123.

42 Cf. C. J. Hemer, *The Book of Acts in the Setting of Hellenistic History* (Tuebingen: 1989), pp. 322–8; A. D. Baum, *Lukas als Historiker der letzten Jesusreise* (Wuppertal and Zuerich: 1993).

43 Lucian of Samosata, *Adversus indoctum* 4.

44 The extent of the persecution under Domitian in AD 95–96, which began as a family affair at court, remains controversial. See, among others, M. Sordi, *The Christians and the Roman Empire* (London and New York: 1994), pp. 43–53, with an analysis of the debate.

45 See Eusebius, *Church History* 6.20.1–2 etc.; cf. Gamble, *Books and Readers in the Early Church* (New Haven and London: 1995), pp. 144–202.
46 Strabo, *Geographica* 14.646.
47 Ignatius, *Philadelphians* 8.2.
48 On average travel times, see M. B. Thompson, 'The Holy Internet: Communication between Churches in the First Christian Generation', in Bauckham (ed.), *The Gospels for All Christians*, pp. 60–5.

7 Test Cases: An Epilogue

1 The tax on fish is documented in Roman sources; cf. Nun, *Ancient Anchorages and Harbours around the Sea of Galilee*, pp. 24–6. It is one of the historical facts which help us to understand the precise number of 153 fish caught by the disciples in John 21.11. Since Simon Peter and the two sons of Zebedee are mentioned explicitly, we know that professional fishermen were in the boat; they were used to counting the fish, so that they could sell their catch properly. But the tax made counting obligatory anyway. Symbolic interpretations of '153' abound, but it is unlikely that John himself, who has been identified by many scholars as John the Son of Zebedee, was thinking in symbols when he recorded a sober observation. Levi-Matthew too, the former *telōnēs*, may have been present, as one of the unnamed disciples (John 21.2). See C. P. Thiede, *Bibelcode und Bibelwort: Die Suche nach verschlüsselten Botschaften in der Heiligen Schrift* (Basel: 1998), pp. 74–81.
2 See C. P. Thiede, 'Schrift VII: Tachygraphie, Kurzschrift', in *Das Grosse Bibellexikon*, vol. 3 (2nd edn Wuppertal and Giessen: 1990), pp. 1401–3; Richards, *The Secretary in the Letters of Paul*, pp. 26–43.
3 On this point, and on the tax and customs office, see W. Wuellner, *The Meaning of 'Fishers of Men'* (Philadelphia: 1967), pp. 22–4; Nun, *Ancient Anchorages in Harbours around the Sea of Galilee*; V. Tzaferis, *Excavations at Capernaum I* (Winona Lake, Ind.: 1989), pp. 2–10.
4 Quoted in Eusebius, *Church History*, 3.39.15–16.
5 For the debate about the imperial tax in Matthew 22.15–22/Mark

12.13–17 as a controversy carried out in Greek, see B. Schwank, 'Ein griechisches Jesuslogion? Ueberlegungen zur Antwort Jesu auf die Steuerfrage', in N. Brox *et al.* (eds), *Anfaenge der Theologie* (Graz: 1987), pp. 61–4; N. Brox *et al.* (eds), 'Wenn Steine zu reden beginnen: Archaeologie zum Verstaendnis des Neuen Testaments', *Bibel und Kirche*, 50 (1995), p. 47.

6 The fiction of 'Q' has led to some weird anomalies in New Testament scholarship. As Mark Goodacre noted, commenting on G. Theissen and A. Merz, *The Historical Jesus: A Comprehensive Guide* (London: 1998), they 'are more willing to discuss doubts about the existence of Jesus than they are doubts about the existence of Q' (M. Goodacre, *The Case Against Q: Studies in Markan Priority and the Synoptic Problem* (Harrisburg, Pa.: 2002), p. 12). Goodacre's study has dealt lethal blows to theories about the existence and contents of 'Q'. The most detailed defence available so far is J. S. Kloppenborg Verbin, *Excavating Q: The History and Setting of the Sayings Gospel* (Minneapolis: 2000). For an analysis of recent 'Q' research, see P. Head and P. J. Williams, 'Q Review', *Tyndale Bulletin*, 54:1 (2003), pp. 119–44.

Luke tells his readers that he knew and used several written and oral (eyewitness) sources (1.2). Apart from late gnostic inventions like the so-called *Gospel of Thomas*, there are early instances of sayings of Jesus not recorded in any of the Gospels – e.g. in Paul's letters, in 1 Peter, and in papyri like P. Egerton 2/P. Koeln Inv.601, dated to *c.* AD 120.

7 See illustrated examples in E. G. Turner, *Greek Manuscripts of the Ancient World*, 2nd edn rev. and enlarged by P. Parsons (London: 1987), pp. 34–5 (nos 6, 7, 8, 10). Cf. M. Hengel, 'The Titles of the Gospels and the Gospel of Mark', in his *Studies in the Gospel of Mark* (London: 1985), pp. 64–84.

8 For example, Papyrus Bodmer II (P66) of John's Gospel, *c.* AD 150.

9 For example, Papyrus Bodmer XIV/XV (P75, with Luke and John, *c.* AD 200, which has the names both above the text and after the final verse.

10 Note also Martin Hengel's verdict: 'There is no trace of such anonymity' (*The Four Gospels and the One Gospel of Jesus Christ* (London: 2000), p. 54).

11 On the identity of the 'Johns' in the New Testament and early

Christianity, cf., among others, J. A. T. Robinson, *The Priority of John* (London: 1985); M. Hengel, *The Johannine Question* (London: 1990); Guthrie, *New Testament Introduction*, pp. 252–82; Carson *et al.*, *An Introduction to the New Testament*, pp. 135–68.

12 On Ignatius, see Chapter 6, n. 26; on the few surviving Papias fragments, see the edition by U. H. J. Koertner, in U. H. J. Koertner and M. Leutzsch (eds), *Schriften des Urchristentums, III: Papiasfragmente. Hirt des Hermas* (Darmstadt: 1998), pp. 3–103.

13 Taking controversial papyri and recent redatings into account, we may have at least seven fragments of the first century: the Qumran documents 7Q4 (1 Timothy) and 7Q5 (Mark), both scrolls of the late fifties to late sixties of the first century; the codex fragments P4 (Luke), P64 and P67 (both Matthew), all mid- to late sixties; P52 (John), late nineties; and the new discovery of a further Matthew Papyrus, P104 (late first or early second century).

14 R. Bauckham, 'For Whom were the Gospels Written?', in Bauckham (ed.), *The Gospels for All Christians*, p. 33.

15 As an historical aside, it should be noted that Peter's Galilean accent is not interpreted as an indication of an uneducated background. Nor is the epithet 'uneducated and ordinary men', applied to the two Galileans Peter and John in Acts 4.13, to be understood in this sense. They were no rabbis, no scribes or members of the Great Sanhedrin: in other words, they did not belong to the 'academic' and priestly elite of their day. And then as much as today, the 'elite' tends to look down on those who do not belong to their circle. That is all there is to it.

16 See Mark 13.35 in the Greek text, and the papyri P37 and P45 for Matthew 26.34.

17 Cf. Claudius Aelianus, *On the Characteristics of Animals* (*c.* AD 200) 3.31.

18 Plato, *Phaedo* 118.

19 Petronius, *Satyrica* 73.6–74.2.

20 Pliny the Younger, *Letters* 10.96.6. For a more general discussion on Pliny's correspondence with Trajan about the Christians, see A. N. Sherwin-White, *The Letters of Pliny: A Historical and Social Commentary* (Oxford: 1966); K. Thraede, 'Noch einmal: Plinius d. J. und die Christen', *Zeitschrift fuer die neutestamentliche Wissenschaft*, 95 (2004), pp. 102–28.

21 Petronius, *Satyrica* 78.2–5.
22 Cf. I. Ramelli, 'Petronio e i Cristiani: allusioni al Vangelo di Marco nel *Satyricon*?', *Aevum*, 70 (1996), pp. 75–80, and *I romanzi antichi e il Cristianesimo: contesto e contatti* (Madrid: 2001), pp. 163–92.
23 Some scholars assume that Chariton's novel is recommended as afternoon reading by Persius, in his *Satires* 1.134, and Persius died on 24 November AD 62. But Persius only mentions the title of a work called 'Callirhoe' ('post prandia Callirhoen do') and we cannot be certain if he was referring to Chariton's novel. See C. P. Thiede, *Ein Fisch fuer den roemischen Kaiser* (Munich: 1998), pp. 127–34; Ramelli prefers a late first-century date for *Chaireas and Callirhoe*: see *I romanzi antichi e il Cristianesimo*, pp. 23–44. In her seminal work, Ramelli discusses further authors of novels and narratives in Graeco-Roman antiquity: Xenophon of Ephesus, Iamblichus, Achilles Tatius, Longus, Heliodorus, Lucian and Apuleius.

Index of Sources

Index of Sources

Index of Subjects

Index of Subjects

emperor worship 34–7
Essenes 80, 91, 111; library 113–15
Ethelwold 29–30
Euripides 27
Eusebius of Caesarea 47, 109–10, 119
Ezekiel the Tragedian 22, 25–7

Festus 131 n.17
forgery 88, 100
Freund, Richard 14

Gadara 42
Gadarene swine 42–7, 58
Gamaliel II, Rabban 112
Gamaliel, Simeon ben 94
Gamla 62
Garden Tomb 47
Gaulanitis 56, 57, 60–3
Gerasa 43–5
Gergesa 43, 45–6
Germanic tribes 10–11
Germanicus 11
Geta 37
Gibson, Mel 75
Glastonbury 3
God-fearers 75, 112
Golan, Oded 86, 88 (147 n.34)
Goodacre, Mark 158 n.6
gospel, meaning of word 49–50
Gospels: authorship 123–4; date 11, 134 n.11;
    literary parodies 126–8
Greek language 11–12, 15, 21, 56, 57, 61, 74;
    on cross 76; and Jews 107–8, 117; on
    ossuaries 82; and tax collectors 121; used by
    first Christians 89–91
Greenhut, Zvi 91–2

Hachlili, Rachel 93
Hananyah, Joshua ben 112
Hanukkah 74
Hauranitis 61
healings 37–40; Gadarene demoniac 42–7
Hebrew language 76
Hegesippus 147 n.35
Hellenization 61–2
Herculaneum 47
Hermopolis Magna 4
Herod Agrippa I 93–4
Herod Antipas 10, 21, 61, 65
Herod the Great 3, 21, 33, 34
Hirbet El Aradsh 60
Honi the Circle-Drawer 39, 40–1
hypocrites 31
Hyrcanos, Eliezer ben 112

Ignatius of Antioch 123–4
imperial cult 34–7
Infancy Story of Thomas 20
ink 101
Ituraea 61

James (brother of Jesus) 85, 88–91
Jamnia, Council 112
Jeremiah 65
Jerome 46, 130–1 n.11
Jerusalem 73–5; Council 89–90; library 119
Jesus of Nazareth: brothers 84; crucifixion
    74–5, 85; date of birth 143 n.10; divinity 41;
    family 130 n.11; flight into Egypt 3; lan-
    guage 11–12, 60, 68, 69, 71, 122; literacy
    120; miracles 41; name 50–1, 70, 85;
    preaching 30–1, 122; as Saviour 36
Jews 2; attendance at theatres 21; education 49,
    54, 78; and emperor worship 34; and
    Greek language 107–8, 117
Joash stele 86, 88
Job 25
John (the Baptist) 63–4, 76
Jonah 68
Joseph (husband of Mary): flight into Egypt 3;
    as landowner 18; trade 15
Joseph of Arimathea 3
Josephus 1, 9, 24
Judas Maccabeus 80
Julia Domna 37
Julius Africanus 119
Justin Martyr 113
Juvenal 24

Kalkriese 9
Kasser, Rodolphe 5

Lamentations 65
Latin language 75, 76
Lemaire, André 86, 147 n.34
Letter of Aristeas 21, 107
letters, writing 99–100
librarians 119
libraries 107–12, 116–18, 119; synagogues 113
Luke 137–8 n.2; Acts 118; Gospel 117–18, 154
    n.26

McCowan, Alec 29
Maoza 19
mariology 130 n.11
Mark, Gospel 117–18
Martial 24, 116
Mary (mother of Jesus) 130 n.11; as landowner
    18–19
Mary's Well 13–14

Index of Subjects

Strato's Tower 33
Strickert, Fred 59
Suetonius 16, 24
Sukenik, Eleazar 82
synagogues 55–6, 74–5, 108, 110–12; libraries
    112, 113

Tacitus 1, 24
Talmon, Shemaryahu 115
tax, on fish 121
tax collectors 121
Temple (Jerusalem) 75
temples (for Augustus) 33–7
Tertullian 23 (132 n.21), 29
textual criticism 135–6 n.23
theatres 21–3; off limits for Christians 23
Theodosius (Archdeacon) 79
Theodotos 74
Theophilus 117–18
Thomas (apostle) 3
Tiberias 21
Tiberius 10, 11
Timothy 100
Tiro 121
Trachonitis 61

Trophimus 75
trumpets 31
Tzetzes, John 153 n.21

Varus, Publius Quinctilius 9–11
Vespasian 34, 38–9
Via Maris 15, 55
Victor, Ulrich 135 n.22
Vitellius 94

West, Martin L. 135–6 n.23
Wilde, Oscar 11–12
Willibald of Wessex 60
Witherington III, Ben 86
writing tablets 97

Yadin, Yigael 113

Zacharias *see* Zechariah
zaddikim 76
Zadok, Elezar Bar 80–1
Zakkai, Yohanan ben 112
Zechariah (father of John the Baptist)
    76–80
Zias, Joseph E. 76, 78–9